Love My Colors

Cleanne Johnson

Dedication

This book is dedicated to my mom, husband, family, and friends, and to all single-parent families of different background, nationality, culture, social class, and ethnicities. This book is dedicated to young girls and boys broken by society's perception of what beauty is supposed to look like.

I encourage you to embrace the self for who you are by loving yourself – it's the greatest gift in which you can shower self. Think and dream big and always give back to your communities, regardless of your upbringing or any harshness that you have encountered at the hands of people.

Things always change as time goes by, it never remains the same. So God will give you the strength to carry through, but always persevere, and in the end, life will be worth it.

Acknowledgment

I want to thank God for His endless love and favor – that He bestowed throughout my life. I thank Him for being my guiding light, my North Star.

About The Author

Cleanne Johnson is a Caribbean-Canadian living in the USA. She completed a Bachelor of Science in dietetics, and a master's in public health at Andrews University in Michigan.

Today, she practices as a registered dietitian and loves to help others make better food choices, to help improve their quality of life.

Preface

This book is for all those people – especially young girls who have been belittled and made fun of, just based on their skin color. Diversity is beautiful, and every skin-color matters – be it black, olive, brown, or white.

Natashia learns to be content in her own skin, with time and a few lessons on the way. Yes, she may be darker-skinned than her mother and the rest of the residents at the island. Yes, she may also be darker-skinned than her lighter-skinned father and the rest of the kids at school… but she is her own person – whatever her skin-color

Contents

Dedication.. i
Acknowledgment ii
About The Author iii
Preface..iv

Chapter 1 – Hole in Heart...1
Chapter 2 – Appearances 20
Chapter 3 – Absentee 39
Chapter 4 – Life in the Island...58
Chapter 5 – Bullying 77
Chapter 6 – The Visit..97
Chapter 7 – Education..113
Chapter 8 – New Beginnings 130
Chapter 9 – Taking a Stance..148
Chapter 10 – England 162
Chapter 11 – The Medical Student.................................180
Chapter 12 – Home 189
Chapter 13 – Robert...201

Chapter 1 – Hole in Heart

A long and angry howl echoed in the small hospital room. It was answered by jubilant, loud cheers by the doctor and nurses who had helped bring this tiny, shrieking baby into the world. Cece watched the time-honored celebration that heralded a new life in this world, smiling but unable to participate. She had just given birth to a daughter whose face she hadn't seen yet. Her own face was puffy and sweaty, and she felt more exhausted than she ever had. Strands of hair stuck to her forehead, and she pushed them back impatiently, signaling to the nurse to bring her newborn so she could hold her.

The nurses told her to wait, so they could clean up the baby properly and check her vitals before handing her to Cece. In that time, Cece thought of the baby's father who wasn't here with her. She'd sorely felt his absence during labor. Neither her family nor his had been able to make it to the city from their respective villages in time. The baby had come earlier than expected. A generous friend had come along with her to the hospital, so she wasn't entirely on her own.

The pangs of loneliness that had overcome her earlier now began to subside. She had her daughter now, and soon; she was going to be with the baby's father, too. Willing back the drowsiness that was starting to engulf her, she thought about the Christmas night, not too far ago, when her life had changed forever.

***

The Christmas party was in full swing inside the large, well-lit hall of the hotel. Cece leaned back against the metal handrails on the verandah where she had retreated to take a breather. She'd attended to hundreds of guests tonight, and the numbers only kept increasing as the night advanced. Behind her, the beach stretched out for miles. The weather was balmy, and a gentle wind was blowing.

Cece felt the coolness of the metal against her bare back. She was wearing a short, backless black dress, which made her feel sophisticated and older than her twenty-two years. Faint music and muffled chatter of the partygoers from inside the hall floated on the air and reached her ears. Through the glass doors, she could see people swinging energetically to the beat of the music.

Surprisingly, she was having a good time tonight, though usually it was just work for her. She worked part-time at the Heritage Park Hotel as a waitress to make some extra money. Deciding to head back, she straightened and put her feet back in the long heels she'd taken off to rest her feet. Just as she was about to go inside, she saw a large man making his way through the glass doors. She had seen him in the hall earlier. He was one of the guests, and he'd caught her eye because he seemed huge to her and also because he was really handsome. She stood at five feet, and this man was well over six feet tall.

He looked at Cece and said in a friendly tone, *"Hello there. I hope I'm not intruding?"*

Cece shook her head and smiled. He extended his hand toward her and said, *"My name is Brad. And what's yours?"*

Taking his large, warm hand, she said, *"I am Cece. I work here at the hotel."*

"Yeah, I saw you back inside. I actually came out here to see you, to be honest. I saw you heading here a while ago." Then he said hesitatingly, *"You're really pretty."*

Cece laughed. She was flattered at his compliment and was clearly enjoying his attention. In those first few moments of flirtation, the two hit it off. Cece talked to him for half an hour, forgetting all about going back to work. He told her he was Lucy's brother and was here with his friends. Lucy worked at the hotel with Cece, though she wasn't here tonight. Realizing it was getting late, Cece went back inside, but not before she arranged to meet Brad again after her shift was over; she still had a few more hours of work left. She was really attracted to Brad and didn't bother to hide it. Neither did him, for that matter.

After the party, the two met up, just like they had planned. In the days that followed, Cece and Brad met each other several times – almost every day. The two of them were from different villages but had been in the city for several years now, so they'd had some shared experience. Brad worked at a construction company and was really ambitious. Cece felt like she had met the man she had always dreamed of but never thought she would find.

He made her laugh and gave her all his attention, as though she was the only person in the world. Walking hand in hand on the beach, going out for late dinners at cafés and dancing in different bars of the city every night, Cece fell in love with Brad. She felt she was the luckiest girl alive when Brad confessed he was in love with her, too. This was the happiest time of Cece's life when all day she daydreamed about her life with him – dreams she knew would turn into reality because things were going great between the two of them. In time, she invited Brad to her village. He was here for the day only and would head to his own village to stay with his parents. The time he spent with her family went well by all appearances.

Brad was quite a charming man who knew how to put people at ease. At the dinner table, conversation flowed as smoothly as the wine. That night, after Brad had left, Cece's mother came to her room, as Cece was getting ready for bed.

Smiling at her mother, Cece said, *"Brad said he really liked you, Mom. He said he had such a good time here!"*

Her mother didn't really react to her excitement. Sitting down on the narrow bed in the room, she said, *"He's quite a sweet-talker, isn't he?"*

Slightly annoyed, Cece turned her back to her mother and resumed looking at herself in the mirror. Brushing her hair, she answered, *"If you mean he's charming then yes, he is that. He is the easiest person to talk to for me."*

Walking to the window, so she could pull apart the curtains, she asked, *"Didn't you like Brad, Mom? I thought you'd love him, which is why I asked him to come here."*

"He's no good, Cece."

Her mom's words made Cece stop dead in her tracks.

She hadn't expected her mom to say such a thing. As far as Cece was concerned, Brad could do no wrong.

Her mom continued, *"Watch this one, Cece. Men like him aren't to be trusted."*

Cece didn't bother correcting her mom or to tell her that she trusted Brad explicitly. She thought she was old enough to know the man she was dating as well as her own mind. A little disapproval from her family wouldn't get in the way of her relationship with Brad. She knew they would come round as time passed and see Brad the way he was, the way she saw him.

When she met Brad's family a few weeks after that, she was pleasantly surprised to see that they all seemed to know everything about her. It was apparent from their excitement that Brad had talked to them about her and that they liked her already, especially his mom. The thought of her own mom's reaction to Brad, and her subsequent 'warning' came to her mind then. She compared her mom's response to Brad with his family's welcoming response toward her. The difference between the two was stark. She didn't let it dampen her good mood, though. After spending a fun weekend at Brad's parents' place, the two of them went back to the city. She had been dating Brad for a few months when she discovered that she was pregnant. The thought didn't really worry her though although she wasn't married to him; she knew he'd be as happy as she was.

That morning, she asked Brad to come to the hotel to pick her up after her shift ended, so she could tell him the news. When she was done with work, she went to the beach at the back of the hotel where Brad was waiting for her at their regular spot. On catching sight of Brad, her face automatically lit up with a huge smile.

Taking his arm, she began walking on the beach with him. To their left, the sea stretched out as far as the eye could see. The horizon seemed to be receding like a mirage. It was the time of sunset, and the sky was the color of burnt leaves. Feeling the still-warm sand under her feet and between her toes, Cece walked silently for a few minutes, arranging her words in just the right order. Around them, many tourists were having a good time at the beach.

Their island was famous for its lagoons and beaches. Walking on the coastline, Cece saw why. The beauty around her was unparalleled. The water of the sea was a clear blue – so much so that it perfectly reflected the sky like a faithful mirror. Finally, she stopped and turned to face Brad, who looked enquiringly at her.

"I wanted to tell you something," she said.

"What is it, Cece?" he asked.

"I'm pregnant. We are going to be parents soon, Brad," she said while watching him closely.

His reaction was better than she expected. He broke into a broad smile and practically shouted, *"What! And you're telling me the news just now?"*

"But I just found out!" Cece said, pleased to no end at his obvious delight.

"I'm so happy, Cece. Now we can have a family of our own," he said.

Then he picked her up and swung her around a few times for good measure to demonstrate just how thrilled he really was. Laughing at his antics, she felt on cloud nine. Could life get any better than this? Her mom was wrong, after all; Brad was nothing like she had thought, and was everything Cece had ever wanted. From that day on, all their conversations revolved around their baby whose arrival would complete their family. Brad had already told her he wanted to marry her, as soon as possible. They couldn't get married though because a few weeks later, Brad was offered a post in England by the same construction company he'd worked at for five years.

It was too good an opportunity to pass. Though Cece didn't want to part from Brad, she didn't try to convince him to stay. Instead, both of them planned for her to join him in England after she had the baby, so they could marry there. Letting go of Brad for a short time was a cost Cece was willing to pay for a good life for herself, and both Brad and her child. Soon, the day came for Brad's departure.

Cece sent him off happily, though she was a little sad at watching him go; she already knew she'd join him soon, so she wasn't really worried about him leaving. Plus, they would be in regular contact with each other. She knew Brad couldn't live without her, as much as she couldn't live without him.

Days passed into weeks and weeks into months. When Cece thought about this time of her life a few years down the line, this period appeared to her to be tinted with rose-gold, it was that dreamy and beautiful. She was full of hopes and plans for the future. She corresponded regularly with Brad through email. She didn't get to talk to him on the phone much because he was really busy and because of the time difference.

During this time, Cece regularly visited Brad's family. In fact, she had grown closer to them than she was to her own family, whose reaction to her pregnancy and plans to join Brad in England was lukewarm at best. Brad's parents, on the other hand, were always extremely happy to see her and now more so, since she was going to give birth to their grandchild soon. Cece had a great relationship with his parents, which, she thought, was wonderful as she would soon marry into their family.

They already treated her like a daughter-in-law, though, and Cece felt special every time she visited them. The day of her child's birth was getting nearer, and she missed Brad all the more. It was still two weeks to the time given to her by the doctors when her baby decided to come into the world. There wasn't time enough to inform her family or his or even

Brad himself. 'Where is Brad, anyway?' She asked herself as she walked behind her friend, who was carrying the bag she'd packed for the hospital to the car. She wasn't really concerned because she knew Brad was usually quite busy, but she thought he at least could have replied to her emails, which he hadn't for a few weeks now. She was patient, however, and knew Brad would contact her as soon as he could. Driving to the hospital, all other thoughts except the impending birth vanished from her mind.

***

Cece was brought back to the present by her crying daughter, who was now swaddled in pink covers and in the arms of the nurse standing to the side of the bed. The baby seemed to have quite a lot of stamina to keep crying for so long, Cece thought to herself. Amused at her judgment, she reached eagerly to take her daughter into her arms. The nurse handed the baby carefully to her, and Cece fussed over holding her, just so before she looked at her properly.

When she saw the baby, however, she let out a soft gasp. She was taken aback for a moment. 'Is this my daughter?' she thought and almost asked the question out loud. 'No, the doctors couldn't have made a mistake like this,' she said to herself silently. The baby in her arms was hers, there was no doubt about it, even though she looked nothing like her or Brad. The point of departure was the color of the baby's skin. In the dim light of the hospital room, it looked as dark as ebony. Neither Cece nor Brad were dark-skinned, so from whom had their baby inherited this complexion? Nevertheless, the baby was hers, and she loved her unconditionally already. In fact, she felt she had loved her daughter, long before she was even born.

Since Brad had not told her what he wanted to name their child, she felt the decision was up to her. She would have to give a name at the hospital, and anyway, she had a really good name in mind: Natashia. So she named her daughter that and took her home. It was there that Brad's parents and her own visited their new granddaughter.

They expressed a bit of shock at Natashia's skin color and joked, *"Are you sure that your daughter didn't get exchanged with someone else's kid at the hospital?"* All in all, though, Cece was happy to see that both sets of grandparents were equally excited at the new addition to their family – even her mom who'd had many reservations about Brad from the start. They helped her with the baby. Ann, Brad's mom, cried a lot on seeing her granddaughter for the first time, though. To Cece, she seemed more emotional than even she was at her daughter's birth; she attributed Ann's tears to a grandparent's love for their grandchild. However, they had to leave and go back home, and she was soon on her own. These were the times when she longed for Brad's presence even more than she already did. It wasn't easy taking care of a newborn all by herself.

She'd expected to be half-way to England by this time – yet, here she was, still waiting for the love of her life to show up from wherever he had disappeared to. There was still no reply from him, though she had emailed him about Natashia's birth as soon as she'd got the chance to. She was starting to get a bit worried now.

What if something had happened to Brad on the construction site? It had never taken him so long to get back to her. The next weekend, she visited Brad's parents and asked them about Brad. They seemed as clueless as she was.

His father said to her, *"He'll be fine, Cece. You don't need to worry about him. I am sure he will write to you soon."*

Cece was somewhat relieved; his parents' confidence made her feel confident, too. A few weeks later, Brad still hadn't replied to any of her emails. When she met Lucy next at the hotel during a break – she had to return to her job soon, as she couldn't afford too long a maternity leave – she asked her if Brad had contacted any of them.

Lucy seemed really uncomfortable at her question, which seemed odd to Cece.

She asked, *"What's wrong, Lucy?"*

"Nothing, really. What could be wrong?" she said with a smile that didn't reach her eyes.

"Where is Brad, Lucy? Why won't you or your parents tell me anything? It's clear that you know where he is," Cece said a bit angrily this time.

Brad's parents' complacency had started to look dubious to her, and now, Lucy's forced manner had made her even more suspicious. She realized they were hiding something from her. But what could it be? What could be so bad that they refused to tell her?

"I have a right to know," Cece said forcefully.

At this, Lucy became even more nervous than she already was. Then, a look of resolve came into her eyes, as if she'd reached a difficult decision.

She said, *"Sit down, Cece."*

The words evoked a strong feeling of dread in Cece. She knew what those words signified – whatever news she was about to receive wouldn't be any good. In those few seconds, a thousand thoughts ran through her mind.

It was as if Lucy's words had set free all of her fears that she'd kept strictly at bay in the last few days when she'd chosen to willfully drown herself in the sense of optimism. The weak wall of optimism, though, had already crumbled. She was prepared to hear the worst.

'So, Brad is dead. Natashia is fatherless now, and I am all alone in the world,' she thought, sitting down on a nearby chair like an obedient child.

"It's about Brad, Cece. I am telling you because you are right, you do have a right to know," Lucy said in a steady voice. All her nervousness seemed to have disappeared.

Cece just wished she'd tell her already. There was no use in prolonging her misery. However, once Lucy told her, she wanted for the clock hands to go back and for the words to retreat back into Lucy's mouth, as though not speaking the truth would make it false.

Lucy said, *"Brad has married someone else in England, Cece."*

Following this announcement, which Cece couldn't have predicted, enveloped in the haze of blind trust and optimism as she was, there was absolute silence. From beyond the bay window, the waves could be seen crashing angrily against the shore. The clock ticked loud enough to be heard, and Cece felt as if her heart would jump right out of her chest, it was beating so hard.

"This can't be true. I am sure Brad would never deceive me like that," she said finally to Lucy in a voice hoarse with the effort to hold back her tears. Even as she said it, she knew what Lucy had told her was true. Lucy wasn't cruel enough to speak a lie of this magnitude.

"It is true, Cece. He married a long time back. He just told us to not tell you till the baby was born. My parents couldn't tell you when they visited you after Natashia's birth. They couldn't bring themselves to."

"Why?" asked Cece, though at this point, she didn't really care why she asked.

"They were ashamed to face you. They feel guilty for what Brad has done to you and now, to Natashia too. You know

they love you. They were so happy when Brad finally seemed to be settling down with you after his 'wild years'. You seemed to be the answer to their prayers," Lucy said earnestly.

"Wild years'?" Cece echoed. She felt disoriented, as though she was emerging out of dense fog after a long, long time.

"You don't know about it? Figures. I wondered why you'd decided to be with Brad despite his history with women. Turns out you didn't know anything at all about him."

"I know what he told me, Lucy. Did he lie to me about everything then?"

"Well, he did lie to you about the kind of man he was. He's had several such relationships with women before, though as far as I know, he never promised to marry any of them like he promised you, Lucy revealed.

"But he was so happy when I told him we were going to have a baby. He wanted to have a family," Cece said hollowly.

"I am sorry, honey, but he's had children with other women before. We don't know where those other kids are

exactly since he never bothered to bring any of the other women to meet the family. But he introduced you to the family, which is why we thought he was finally serious about someone. But I guess a leopard cannot change its spots," she said cynically. She seemed as disgusted with her brother as Cece felt.

After that, there wasn't anything left to stay. Cece silently got up from the chair and placed the hand cloth with which she was cleaning the counter before her world came crashing down on her head. Not caring about work, she walked out of the hotel. On her way to pick up Natashia, her brain was assaulted with hundreds of conflicting thoughts.

She thought how though Brad was alive, he was as good as dead to her. She thought about how Natashia would have to grow up without a father. She thought how she would meet her mother's eyes now, which would scream 'I told you so' loud and clear even if she refrained from saying the words out loud.

She thought how her life, as she knew it, was over.

Most of all, she thought of ways to get back at Brad for what he had done to her.

Even as these thoughts rolled through her mind like a strong, sickening storm that threatened to destroy all in its path, she knew she would have to put herself second. Her life had changed irrevocably after the birth of her daughter. She knew no matter how enraged and mad for vengeance she was, her main goal in life would be to bring up her daughter well.

That responsibility was all hers now, she thought bitterly, as visions of those beautiful dreams of a family passed before her eyes, as though to mock her. As images from the past invaded her mind, she resolutely pushed them away. It was in those moments, the most horrible moments of her life, that she resolved to give her daughter a good life – the best life that she could. And that, she decided, would be her revenge.

Chapter 2 – Appearances

Claiming to forget a person and really forgetting them were two different things entirely, as Cece discovered in the days following Natashia's birth. Brad's betrayal had cut in too deep for her to forget it so easily. She had trusted him blindly, and he had stabbed her in the back. Even so, for many days after she had learned of his deception, she kept thinking about him. Sometimes, in the middle of the day, she'd catch herself falling into the old daydreams of being with Brad in England with their daughter with them. It had become a habit for her: her dreams got her through the day, but now the harsh reality shone on her like a merciless sun.

There was no shade for her to take cover. Cece had decided to raise Natashia on her own, but that, too, was a task easier said than done. Growing accustomed to life as a mother – and a single parent, as well – was not precisely a piece of cake. There were things she knew nothing about raising a child, but which she had thought she would manage with Brad by her side. That was not to be anymore, however, and she knew she had to carry the responsibility on her own shoulders.

It would have been challenging with any child, but it was even more so with Natashia. And the reason for that was Natashia's appearance.

"Why does she look like that, Cece?" her mother had asked her concernedly when she had first seen Natashia.

"I don't know, Mom. But she looks the way she looks. What can I do about it?" Cece had answered as though she didn't care a whit about what her mother had said.

From all appearances, Cece had dismissed her mother's words from her mind. However, the truth was that her words had kept echoing in Cece's mind for long afterward. If her own mother, Natashia's grandmother who loved her despite what she saw and said, had not hesitated from voicing her thoughts on how Natashia looked, could Cece really expect the world to remain silent?

In those moments when Cece had held Natashia in her arms for the first time, instead of being overwhelmed by feelings of love, she was assaulted by feelings of apprehension. The reason for that was Natashia's skin color was black. She was a dark-skinned baby, who looked nothing like her parents did. This is why Cece had had to endure jokes of her daughter being exchanged with someone else's baby from the time that Natashia was born. Cece had laughed at those jokes but only to get along. She didn't really find them funny. The village she came from had quite restricted standards of beauty. At the time of Natashia's birth, Cece had already accepted the fact that her daughter would never fit in the society she was born into. She knew that the people she lived with admired fair skin with a fervor that never seemed to allow for any deviations.

Anyone who looked different than the standard they had decided for beauty was deemed as an anomaly and was henceforth treated almost as an outcast. Cece didn't want her daughter to grow up in such a place which would not accept her – and merely because she was dark-skinned. There was nothing she could do about it, however, except wait to see how things played out as Natashia grew up. She could only hope it wouldn't be too bad.

Days blurred into years, and soon, Natashia was three years old. In that time, Cece grew up more than she ever thought she would. The responsibility of being a single parent to her daughter had made her stronger than she had ever imagined she would be. After Natashia's birth, Cece could no longer work in the city. She needed someone to care for the baby while she went to work, and there was no one there to help her with her child. So she moved back to her village where she lived with her sisters and mother, who looked after Natashia while she was off to work. Natashia was a bright and active child who ran around tirelessly all day. Cece sometimes wondered where she got all her energy from – she herself was drained every day after getting home from a long day of work. Then she reminded herself that she was an adult while Natashia was a child, blissfully isolated from the harsh realities of life. She didn't even know her father was missing, though Cece believed she would soon begin to ask questions.

She was approaching the age where children watch other families and start to compare and question. Cece was wholly unprepared to give her any answers – at least, not the ones that would satisfy her. Their house was located up a steep hill. A long, narrow road led to it, which non-locals would find hard to climb in ordinary days. Yet there was Natashia, who ran up the hill like a little goat. This was all the world that the little girl knew, and she was happy here. It was Cece who was even now, in her unguarded moments, tortured by what could have been, in place of what really was her and her daughter's life.

Brad had married someone from his own village, and in the first few months, after she had become aware of his betrayal, she had been driven to find out as much as she could about the woman. It appeared to her that Brad hadn't really known her or had dated her before; he had only married her, to the surprise of his own family, once he got to England. In time, Cece had given up obsessing over Brad and his marriage. She had, for the most part, accepted things as they were and was busy bringing up her daughter.

"Natashia, come inside!" hollered Cece one day, as it rained non-stop in the village.

"In a minute, Mommy!" answered Natashia in her high-pitched, childlike voice.

She was, at this time, busy alternating between climbing up the mango and plum trees that lined their small yard. Their house, which could be called a rudimentary house at best, was located on a picturesque site, which overlooked a grove of coconut, mango, and plum trees. Natashia was habitual of plucking the fruits from the trees and eating them fresh. Even now, she was swinging from branch to branch – or at least, she was trying to – as though she were Tarzan.

"Help Mommy with all the water that's coming in, honey. Come on, Mommy needs help," Cece said in a loud voice.

This time the child did not argue but made her way through the main door of the small house. She saw the scene before her and shook her head in the manner of a wise old granny who has seen so much of the world that nothing, however extraordinary or appalling, surprised her anymore. What she saw before her, indeed, was something she had seen growing up every time it rained. The galvanized roof of their house, browbeaten into submission by age and weather long ago, now sported several holes in different locations.

Water was dripping in through those holes now, and it seemed as if the rain didn't stop soon, the entire house would be flooded. Natashia pulled up her skirt, which really wasn't that long, and waded slowly through the layer of water that had already accumulated. Cece had called her in to help her stem the water inflow, something that they had to do every time it rained. They, at present, just did not have enough money to get the roof fixed. Natashia knew what she had to do. She walked over to the wood shelf at the corner of the small kitchen and retrieved several small buckets from the bottom rack.

Then she ran around the house, putting those buckets beneath all the places the roof leaked. The rooms were now full of a merry tune: the drip-drip-drip of rain falling into the plastic containers. This, added to the rain pattering on the roof, provided the mother-daughter duo with background music to which they finished completing the remaining household chores. When the buckets became full, as they did in some time, Natashia collected them from the room and went outside to throw away the water.

The other residents of the house, two of Cece's sisters, were not home yet. And it had still not stopped raining. As Natashia came back inside with the buckets, Cece saw they weren't all empty: one of them had quite a collection of the plums that had, no doubt, fallen from the trees by the force of the wind that accompanied the rain. Giggling happily, Natashia said by way of explanation, *"This is for the pigs, Mommy. You know, the ones at Lena's house."* At this age, Natashia had a lisp, which made her efforts at conversation very endearing to those who heard. She was referring to her older cousin who lived down the street barely five miles away and had several pigs, who Natashia loved to visit from time to time.

Cece didn't scold her for it, and let her keep the plums for the pigs. Such little things made her daughter very happy, and she didn't like taking away the things that made her smile. As it was, Cece constantly berated herself for not providing for Natashia in a better way, even though she did all that she could. It just wasn't easy making ends meet with the poor job opportunities available in the vicinity of their village. Everyone in their village, which was called the Gebo land, not only knew each other but were also related to one another in near or distant ways.

This was because a large swath of this region was the property of Cece's great-great-grandmother. It was given to her after slavery on the island was abolished. Later, she had distributed the land amongst her offspring whose descendants to this day lived here, though there was no proper system of electricity and water supply here. Even though it felt like a backwater place after having lived in the city to Cece, she was happy that her daughter at least was growing up amongst family.

Even Brad's parents, who loved their granddaughter, visited them from time to time. There was always a look of contrition on their faces, and it was obvious that they were ashamed of what their son had done. Cece didn't fault them for his doings, though, and only had goodwill toward his parents who had always treated her nicely. A few days after the heavy rain, Cece took Natashia to visit her great-grandmother Sasa who lived two miles up the hill on a steeper slope. From her home, you could see far into the distance on clear days and even make out the island that lay in the west. The old woman was delighted to see them like she always was.

She had wiry white hair that was so puffy that it seemed like there was a halo around her head. She didn't know English, so Natashia had learned to speak English-based Creole automatically, as the old lady always talked to her in that language. Opening her arms to Natashia, she enveloped the little girl in a warm hug. Then she hugged Cece and asked her how things were going.

"Grandma! I want sweets!" chimed in Natashia before Cece could respond.

Cece rolled her eyes at Natashia's impatience – really, the child didn't even pretend she had come to visit for anything other than the sweets that her great-grandmother always offered her – and told her to quiet down for a while so that the two grownups could catch up with each other. Natashia pulled a face at being scolded. Then she proceeded to cross her arms tightly across her small body, as she stared grumpily at the wall, pointedly ignoring her mother and great-grandmother. The two women watched her with amusement as she pouted and puckered her lips, hoping to get noticed, even though she made a great show of anger at being disregarded. The older woman, laughing, gave in to the child's adorable antics.

"Here, come here, my girl. Come take your sweets," she said with a twinkle in her eyes.

Natashia only needed those few words. She jumped from her seat, forgetting all about being angry, and danced her way to her great-grandmother. Reaching inside the bodice of her blouse, Sasa retrieved the small white pouch from inside her bra where she usually hid it. Then she opened the pouch to reveal the many multi-colored sweets inside.

"Now, have just a few of these. We don't want your teeth to rot, do we?" Sasa said to Natashia who bobbed her tiny head vigorously in assent. Sprinkling some of the sweets on Natashia's hand, the old woman got up from her chair with her hands on her knees for support. She took the walking cane she always used and headed to the kitchen to brew some

coffee. She was a certified caffeine addict who couldn't live without her daily dose of coffee, which was quite higher than average. For Natashia, she brewed 4 oz. of decaffeinated coffee; she then added a tablespoon of sugar and condensed milk to it. The thing was that Natashia wanted to do everything that she saw adults around her doing, but they obviously couldn't give her caffeine.

So this was the alternate they had come up with to satisfy the ever-curious child. Handing her cup of coffee to her with a flourish as though she were a princess being served by a peasant, the old lady got a giggle out of Natashia that made her very happy. Then sending the child off to entertain herself, she sat down with Cece.

"How is work, Cece?" she asked.

"It's okay, grandma. The same as ever," Cece said in a normal tone of voice. She seemed resigned to her circumstances.

"Natashia is growing up…" Sasa said, hinting toward something that Cece didn't understand.

"Yes, she is. She's already three years old!" Cece said a little breathlessly, as though amazed anew at the fact that her daughter had grown up so fast.

"What I mean is, soon she's going to start asking questions..." Sasa added.

"She already asks a lot of questions, grandma. Just last night she was asking me where the stars go during the day and if where they go is the same place where the sun hides at night," Cece laughed.

Sasa smiled at that. Natashia was a bit of a precocious child. This became apparent when she imitated all those who were older than her. This was why she would have coffee like her great-grandmother, say her mind like her grandmother, cross her legs when she sat like her mother did, and climb trees and run around in her bare feet like all her older cousins were in the habit of doing. Most of them indulged her because Natashia was the youngest in the family and also because seeing her copy them was enjoyable for them.

"I don't mean those questions, Cece," Sasa decided to be direct about it. *"I mean she will start asking about her father. What do you plan to tell her?"*

The color drained from Cece's face. Even after all this time, any questions regarding Natashia's father hurt her. She didn't have an answer ready for her grandmother, so she only said, *"We'll cross that bridge when we come to it, grandma. I'll find something to tell her."*

After that, Sasa didn't pursue the subject. She could see Cece was disturbed, and she didn't want to upset her anymore. They whiled away the time, exchanging harmless gossip and commenting on the unpredictable weather conditions of their village till it was time for Cece and Natashia to go home.

***

Traipsing up the narrow pathway up the hill on her way back from her cousins' place, Natashia saw they had visitors. Their small house seemed crowded from a distance. Her curiosity piqued, Natashia ran up the hill. She burst through the door of their house, startling the guests. The guest, actually – there was only the one man. He wore cowboy boots. His long legs were encased in tight jeans, and there was a large hat on his head that hid most of his face.

On seeing Natashia enter the house, he stood up from his seat on the old rickety chair and approached her. He was so huge that he seemed like a giant to Natashia. As he got near, she felt dwarfed by him. Panicking at the sight of the strange man advancing toward her, she retreated her steps and looked around for her mother. She spotted Cece standing near the entrance of the small passageway that led to the kitchen. She ran toward Cece and wrapped her arms around her legs.

Then she got behind her for protection and peeked around her to see whether the strange man was still there. He was. He took off his large hat, which finally revealed his face to Natashia. She saw that she had never met the man before, and he was a stranger just like she had thought. He had lighter skin unlike her, and looked like an exotic traveler to her, dressed as he was in fancy clothes that marked him out as a tourist.

"Is this her?" he asked her mother for confirmation, his eyes widening as though he had seen a particularly rare oddity at a museum. Her mother jerked her head in assent, not bothering to say anything.

The big man turned toward her. He stared at her for a good long minute, scrutinizing her face for who knows what trace or proof. Then he pulled his lips apart in a smile that seemed more like a grimace, revealing a set of perfect white teeth that shone in his white face nevertheless. Natashia continued to stare at him without smiling.

Then he said, *"Hi, Natasha. I am Brad. Has your mom told you about me?"* He didn't pronounce her name correctly, Cece noticed.

Natashia looked up at her mom. She was old enough to understand the words being said but not to know what they implied. Her mother stared fixedly at the man. Her face seemed to be set in stone, but to Natashia, it seemed as if there were lines of anger etched around her mouth and eyes, just like they were when Natashia disobeyed her one time too many.

"Cece, you have to introduce me to her," he said to Cece. *"The child obviously has no knowledge of who I am or who I should be. So don't make it any harder than it already is."*

Cece wanted to scream at him. She wanted to hurl the coffee mug that rested on the small table in the room at his head for good measure. She wanted to tell him he had no right to barge into their home three years too late, and no right to order her about as to what she should or shouldn't tell her own daughter – the one she had raised up on her own. But instead of doing any of that, she reined in her temper and swallowed her rage like a bitter medicine. When she spoke, this is what she said, *"Natashia. Her name is Natashia, not Natasha."*

Without waiting for him to answer, she reached around to grab her daughter by her arm and pulled her from behind her so that Brad could look at her clearly. *"Stand straight, Natashia,"* said Cece in a somber, no-nonsense manner. At this point, Natashia knew enough to not play around. She knew her mother was in a serious mood and wouldn't tolerate any disobedience. So she stood straight up, just like her mother had taught her.

"This is your father, Natashia. Brad, this is your daughter," Cece said brusquely.

At this, Natashia turned to look thoroughly at the man who was looking at her with the same smile, which seemed more and more like it belonged to someone else's face and not his. She knew what 'father' meant. She also knew that this strange man who she had never seen before and who had never in her life taken her out to play and who had never swung her high up in the air and who stared at her as though she were an animal inside the zoo and not a little girl who loved mangoes and coffee and sweets was not her father. He could not be her father. She knew that so she didn't bother pretending otherwise and said loudly, *"This man is not my father, Mommy."*

Her supposed 'father' shook his head at Natashia's stubborn statement and contradicted her by saying, *"I am your father, honey. Doesn't mommy say so? I have come all the way to Gebo to see you!"*

"He seems so proud of the fact that he's come here, and now wants everyone to fall to his feet or if not that, than to cheer him on like a war hero for the great effort he had made to be here," Cece thought sarcastically.

She saw him strut toward Natashia with the same confidence she had always seen him demonstrate – the confidence that he'd be accepted wholeheartedly and unreservedly by whomever he decided to pay his attention to. He reached toward Natashia and clutched her thin arms, apparently to pick her up. It didn't go as he had planned.

Natashia kicked out her legs as soon as he got hold of her and surprised at this unanticipated reaction, he let her go at once. She stomped on his foot two or three times, as she cursed a blue streak in English-based Creole and English. Then she marched away inside and shut the door behind her, as Brad watched her with his mouth open in shock. Cece smiled quietly to herself. She hadn't taught Natashia to behave this way, but the fact that she had made her infinitely glad. Turning toward Brad, she told him she needed time to acquaint Natashia with this new presence in her life. She wanted him gone as soon as possible, but he didn't leave. Her sisters and Natashia's cousins came home. Natashia came out then to play with them.

As Brad made small talk with Cece's family, who were polite to him since he was a guest, he watched his daughter play around with her cousins. She seemed entirely unbothered and ignored his presence, as though he didn't exist for her. Brad could see that his own daughter had rejected him; she obviously needed time to place him as her father in her life. On her part, Cece watched both Brad and Natashia. She hid her feelings of pain and resentment against Brad.

She didn't want to demean herself by letting him know she was still hurt by what he had done years ago. The man was unwilling to be repentant and acted as though he hadn't done anything wrong. As he left their house an hour later, he added insult to injury by handing Cece a hundred-pound bill.

Cece was so shocked that she didn't react and took the currency note from him. When she came to her senses, she wanted to tear it into several pieces and hurl it at his face. It was nothing less than he deserved for thinking he could make up for all the lost time and tears and energy and expenses that Cece had been responsible for in the three years since Natashia was born.

On second thought, it was nothing less than she expected of a man who had left her to give birth to his daughter on her own, who had never bothered to inform her of his marriage to another woman, and who had never, in the three years, contacted her to ask about his own child. She stomped down on all her feelings of bitterness with a hard resolve. Then she thought about the way Natashia had 'welcomed' Brad. The thought brought a smile to her face. She couldn't wait to tell her sisters about this incident and already looked forward to their reactions.

Chapter 3 – Absentee

"It was one of the most satisfying moments of my life!" Cece laughed as she related the incident with Brad to her sister Mary.

"Though Natashia is too young to know or understand anything about her dad, she just disliked him at first sight. And she wasn't shy to tell him exactly what she thought of him!"

"I am glad! At least that good-for-nothing scum knows the reputation he has in these parts of the island," Mary said in a sarcastic tone.

"At least, my daughter has a better grasp of what people are really like underneath their pretty face. The instinct of a child amazes me," Cece concluded.

She was indescribably happy at how Natashia had told Brad off. She did not seem to be in the mood of keeping quiet about it anytime soon.

For her part, Natashia soon forgot about the man who had visited them and who she had so disliked. Life went on for her the same way that it always did, and the appearance and the subsequent disappearance of a strange man in no way affected her. Brad went back to England to his new family, and that was that about him. Cece was relieved to have him gone. She didn't think she could deal with his presence in her and her daughter's life for very long. Looking at him after all these years had opened the floodgates of memory, and she really did not want to descend back into that dark hole from where she had emerged with considerable effort and difficulty.

During this time, there was a British woman named Alice Robert, who came for an indefinite stay on the island. Cece came to know about it and quickly applied to work as a maid for her. Natashia was still young, and Cece didn't know where to leave her for the day, as the job consisted of long hours – from morning till evening. So she decided to take Natashia with her on her first day to keep an eye on her. She knew her daughter could very well get into trouble if left on her own, as she had a knack of doing precisely that; hiring a babysitter was out of the question since Cece couldn't afford one.

"Hello. Cece, is it?" the white lady who was to be her employer now asked Cece, as she entered through the gates of the large house.

"Yes, ma'am," Cece said politely.

"And who do we have there? Let's see," she said brightly as she spotted Natashia standing behind Cece.

The truth was that Cece had strictly instructed her to remain standing quietly behind her while she talked to the white lady. Natashia was more likely to leap about and run around Cece's new employer's house than remain quiet like a shy little girl. Cece, however, wanted to make an excellent first impression. For this to happen, she believed that not only herself but even Natashia would have to be on her best behavior.

"It's my daughter. Her name is Natashia," Cece said by way of introduction. *"Come say hello to Mrs. Robert, Natashia."*

At this, Natashia first stared at her mother and then at the new lady who she had seen for the first time in her life, but who appeared nice, smiling sweetly at her as she was.

Then, to Cece's embarrassment, she said, *"I can't come out from behind you, Mama. Remember you told me not to do that at the white lady's house?"*

Then, without waiting for Cece's answer who was actually left speechless at her child's typical honesty and no-

nonsense way of talking, Natashia turned to the Mrs. Robert and said with her characteristic candor, *"Mama told me not to stare at you, not to run around your house, not to jump on sofas, and to remain very, very quiet. Just like a mouse, you know?"*

"A mouse?" Mrs. Robert said in a tone that indicated she was highly amused.

"Yes, mouse! We sometimes have a brown mouse visit us at our house, and he walks very quietly to get all the food because he doesn't want us to hear!" Natashia kindly explained.

During this revealing monologue which Cece was entirely unprepared for, the white woman stared at the little girl with widening eyes. Cece acutely felt her mistake of letting Natashia tag along and that, too, on the first day of the job. She was relieved, however, when Mrs. Robert let out a delightful laugh at the end of Natashia's speech.

"Your daughter is so precious, Cece! I am glad you brought her with you. She seems to be a bright and funny child to me. I have three kids of my own. Two sons and a daughter! My youngest is actually just a few months old; we call him Moses. I hope, Cece, you can also help me take care

of him. It does get hard to bring up three small children on my own. In the meantime, Natashia here can keep herself busy by playing with the two older kids while you work," she said. Cece smiled. She was pleased to have heard good things about her daughter for once. She also loved that the lady had invited Natashia to play with her kids, rather than asking Cece to leave her daughter at home from the next day.

Ever since Natashia was born, she had brought her to this island. People just seemed to have never noticed how smart and cheerful her daughter was – at least, no one outside the family had. They all noticed her appearance and never chose to look beyond it. Sometimes, Cece was amazed at how prejudiced and blind people can be to be fixated on the skin color of someone – and a child, no less – and not see the beauty within.

The day progressed, and Cece worked her way through the house with Mrs. Robert, who trained her how to go about cleaning and maintaining the household. It was a considerable responsibility, but Cece was happy to take it on since the job paid well. Natashia, too, learned how to go about her day at Mrs. Robert's house. She quickly made friends with Tim and Olive and spent the entire day running around in the garden with them.

Cece watched her through the window from time to time, to make sure she didn't get too excited and scare the new kids off; she was happy to see that Natashia didn't experience any difficulties in connecting with the two children, though they were from different cultures. Till now, Natashia had only been around her cousins, who had known her since she was born. She hadn't started school yet and had had no encounters with unfamiliar faces.

Today, however, she had been introduced to new people, and Cece was glad to see that Natashia was her usual happy and energetic self with them. She was also relieved that the white kids displayed no discrimination against Natashia for her skin color. Looking at these children, she couldn't help but marvel at a child's innocence not yet marred by the society's bigoted ways. If only the grownups were as pure-hearted as these little kids!

Later that night, as Cece sat with her sister after having dinner and putting Natashia to sleep, she shared her thoughts with her.

"The white woman is extremely kind. She let me work at my pace and didn't treat me like I was her slave like these

people usually do. The best thing about her, though, was that she let Natashia play with her kids."

Mary's raised her brows in surprise at that and said, *"That is really surprising. I did not expect that to happen."*

"Yeah, me neither. I mean, the best that I hoped for was that she'd let me keep Natashia there with me. I hadn't expected her to let Natashia mingle with her kids. There is the class difference between us and also, the racial difference. Most foreigners are wary of letting their kids socialize with the locals, especially their servants' children," Cece answered.

"I hope it does Natashia good, though. The child does run a bit too wild, Cece," Mary said, a bit hesitantly.

She knew her sister was a little sensitive about her daughter, and so, she never said anything that might hurt her feelings.

Cece, however, said in response, *"I know that, Mary. I am thinking about what I should do about it. She's growing up now. I want her to be a well-behaved child who knows right from wrong. Being a single mother, it's especially hard. I don't want people to raise their fingers at my daughter when she grows up. She doesn't have her father to protect her. She needs to learn to carry herself properly, or others will make life very difficult for her."*

Mary knew what went on in her sister's mind all the time. Ever since her daughter's birth and Brad's deception and abandonment, Cece was no longer the girl she knew. She wasn't carefree, and she wasn't playful like she had been before. There was always the burden of responsibility on her head. In some ways, Mary knew Cece felt like a failure – for not being able to keep her daughter's father with them and for not being able to provide her daughter with a better life.

Even though Cece knew Brad was a no-good two-timer, and she had nothing but contempt for him now, it still rankled her to have gone through what she had because she was too blind to see the signs. The truth about Brad didn't stop her from beating herself up about falling for him in the first place. After Brad's desertion, she had become a serious woman whose first priority was the proper upbringing of her child and not her own life and personal interests.

As they turned off the lights and prepared to go to sleep, Mary only hoped things would work out well for her sister and her niece. They'd already seen enough bad things in life to last them a lifetime. The days progressed, and Cece settled into her new job at Mrs. Robert's house. Natashia, too, settled right in as though she belonged there. All through the day, she'd follow the same routine as the Robert kids. Cece would have her eat breakfast at home, but during lunch time, she'd sit at the table with Tim and Olive and eat with them. She'd then play with Olive's dolls and even take baths together with her.

Cece had found out a way to keep Natashia in check: every day she gave two cookies to Natashia if she was a good girl. Cece never asked Mrs. Robert about taking cookies from her kitchen for some reason, and by the time it occurred to her that she should have asked for her permission before taking cookies for her daughter, it was somehow too late. The promise of the treat kept Natashia somewhat calm. Otherwise, Cece knew she'd run around like a terror and wreak havoc in the house she'd just spent the entire day putting in order.

Things took a different turn one day when Cece took Natashia to the house with her as usual. Natashia spent the entire morning playing hide and seek with Olive and Tim. The three had run amok and had used every nook and cranny of the house as a hiding spot. They hid behind curtains, underneath beds, at the back of the couch, and in the tiny space between the living room sofas. Natashia, however, had taken it a step further and had tried climbing into a cupboard left open by the cleaning help. Cece was grateful she had spotted her child trying to maneuver herself into the small space. If she hadn't, who knows how long it'd have taken for them to find her? After that, Cece had put a stop to the game. This did not deter Natashia, who then diverted all her energies to get her hands on Baby Moses. She begged Mrs. Robert in her wheedling voice to let her hold the baby.

She said, *"I am just going to hold him for a minute, Mrs. Robert. He likes playing with me!"*

Mrs. Robert had relented, and though Natashia was small herself, she let her hold the baby. Cece watched as Natashia carefully cradled the baby's head against her shoulder and tried lulling the baby to sleep by singing a folk song she had learned from Sasa. Mrs. Robert was endlessly amused by Natashia, and laughed when the baby only stayed wide-awake, even after Natashia's ministrations. Cece, on her part, knew what would be coming next. She knew her daughter enough to predict that sooner or later, Natashia would be coming up to her with a demand to have a baby of their own at home. She was already thinking of excuses to present to her daughter when the time came for it.

It was in the evening that Natashia did something that genuinely embarrassed Cece like she had never been before in her life. What happened was that Cece forgot to give Natashia her usual share of cookies for the day. She had been distracted all day by the baby, who would not go to sleep no matter what she tried. The baby kept fussing, and Cece was running out of patience, with her daughter as well who kept pestering her for the cookies. Natashia waited and waited, but the time came for them to leave, and still, there were no cookies. So she stomped her foot and said impatiently, *"Where are my cookies?"*

She was frowning, and she had raised her voice. Mrs. Robert heard her. Cece saw as there appeared a question in her eyes, but just then, Natashia caught Mrs. Robert's hand and led her inside the kitchen. Cece followed and saw from the doorway, as Natashia indicated the top cabinet where the cookie jar was kept. She told Mrs. Robert, that's where her Mama got her cookies every day, but today she had forgotten so Mrs. Robert could give her the cookies instead. Mrs. Robert smiled and retrieved the cookie jar from the top shelf. Instead of two cookies, she gave Natashia four cookies. She also didn't say a word to Cece.

However, Cece felt guilty for doing what she had. Now Mrs. Robert knew she had been handing out cookies to her daughter without letting her know, let alone asking for her permission. She panicked, thinking Mrs. Robert might label her as a thief, as someone who stole from her employer regularly. She said nothing to Mrs. Robert, however. Soon after that, she left her house taking Natashia's hand in hers, hoping she hadn't lost her job.

She was too embarrassed to even apologize to Mrs. Robert. The only hope she had, at this point, was that Mrs. Robert wouldn't fire her for this misstep. She prayed in her heart for that to not happen. Losing this job was something that she could not afford at all at this point in her life. The next day, Cece showed up to work with dread weighing her down.

However, Mrs. Robert treated her like usual, as though nothing out of the ordinary had happened. Cece felt more mortified than before – it was written all over her face. She was sure Mrs. Robert saw it and understood; she vowed never to do such a stupid thing again. She was extremely grateful to Mrs. Robert for not calling her out on what she realized was the wrong thing to do. It was that day that she decided to enroll Natashia at preschool. It was time that she learned how to behave with people who were not family. It wasn't easy for Cece to collect the funds needed to put Natashia in school. She still had some of the money Brad had given to her the night he had visited them. She reluctantly used it but needed more. As always, her family pitched in. Her sister loaned her some money. Two of Natashia's cousins – Jack and Nancy – had already started preschool at the same institute so that's where Cece enrolled Natashia with firm hopes that it would give a good foundation to Natashia's educational career. This is how the next stage of her daughter's life began.

"Why is that woman lying on the bed, Mama? Is she sleeping?" Natashia leaped up and down, as Cece held her hand, trying to get a good look at the front of the classroom.

She had just entered her first ever classroom in life and was surprised to find a bed there – and a woman resting on it. The scene reminded Natashia of when Grandma Sasa had once unexpectedly fallen ill. That's how she had looked when Natashia had gone to visit her – tired and sleepy so much so that she hadn't even gotten up from the bed to greet Natashia or give her one of the candies that she always did. Cece told her to keep quiet and be a good little girl. She also told her to not point or whisper about the lady at the front of the class because that was her teacher. Cece soon left Natashia in the care of the class teacher. It was perhaps for the first time that Natasha went so long without her mother to attend to her, yet she didn't cry or create trouble like most kids her age are likely to do. She was, by nature, a curious child. So she spent her time looking at the other kids, smiling at them, and making friends by playing games with them.

It was also a fact that Natashia was totally enamored by her new teacher, who looked like a novelty to her. The teacher smiled as she taught them from her position in bed, but she was also quite strict. She told Natashia three times to leave her shoes at the door till Natashia finally understood she had to follow whatever the teacher told her to. This was the time that she finally learned the island rule of never entering someone's house with your shoes on.

Though Cece had tried teaching her that, she kept forgetting. When her teacher taught her that – well, it was a different matter entirely. Natashia knew instinctively not to play around with the teacher, Mrs. Boyce. Though she never once raised her voice to the kids, there was a steely undertone to her words when she spoke, and a firm look in her eyes that told Natashia no disobedience would be tolerated. It was a look that Grandma Sasa got in her eyes when she wanted Natashia to do as she told. Days passed, and Natashia settled into her routine at the school. Cece was pleased to see that Natashia was good at studies. She also liked studying as much as she loved playing. Cece knew that from the fact that every day Natashia got home from school, she'd take out her books in the evening and show Cece all the work she had done that day. She'd go over the new things she'd learned and read out the alphabets and the numbers like a little parrot.

There was one thing; however, that kept bothering Cece. It was that Natashia had started to ask questions about her father. She had obviously seen her new friends with their fathers and wanted to know why she didn't have one. The last time she had asked, Cece had changed the topic. She didn't know how long she could continue to put off Natashia's questions. It was a typical hot and humid day on the island that Cece decided to give Natashia a treat. She had done particularly well on her math assignment, and the teachers had given her three golden stars that signified 'excellent work'. Cece was pleased beyond measure. The ice-cream cart was at its usual spot by the park near the village center.

As they got off the minibus, Natashia squealed excitedly and began to drag Cece to the cart: *"Look, Mama, look! There he is! The ice-cream man!"*

"I can see that, Natashia," Cece said with a smile. Looking at her happy child made her happy, too, and she was glad to have set aside some money for giving this little treat to her daughter.

"How much is the ice-cream?" she asked the vendor. *"It costs 75 cents a cone, madam,"* he answered.

"We'll take two of those," Cece said. Then she turned to Natashia and prodded her with her arm, *"What do we have to say to this gentleman, Natashia?"*

Natashia quickly screamed, *"Thank you!"*

Cece smiled, proud that her daughter had learned manners in the short time she had spent at school. The vendor handed out a vanilla cone to Cece and thinking that Natashia would want chocolate ice-cream like most children do, she kept the vanilla cone for herself. As the vendor was preparing the cone for Natashia, Cece licked her cone and sighed at the cool sweetness that melted in her mouth. She was jolted out of her happy mood when Natashia began to yell out of nowhere.

"That was mine, Mama! That was my ice-cream!" the little girl screamed as loud as she could.

"Here is your ice-cream, little madam," the vendor said politely, handing out the chocolate cone to Natashia.

"No! I don't want this!" Natashia yelled, taking the cone and throwing it to the ground.

Cece was dumbstruck by this unwarranted show of anger on Natashia's part. Here she was, marveling at her child's good behavior a minute ago, and now out of blue Natashia had thrown a tantrum like she never had before. Cece really lost her cool when Natashia proceeded to stamp furiously on the cone that was now melting on the ground.

In disbelief, she heard the ice-cream vendor shake his head and say, *"ill-mannered child."*

Cece yanked Natashia by her arm and then bring her closer, she proceeded to spank the child one and then two and then three times. Natashia displayed an incredible amount of stubbornness by not crying even once. She just looked defiantly at her mother, as though daring to hit her again. Cece saw and understood the signs of rebellion that her daughter was displaying.

Profusely apologizing to the vendor, she paid for the two cones and headed home, dragging Natashia behind her to the bus stop. Taking the next minibus home, she knew that the day was ruined. Cece was disappointed beyond measure, but worse was the fact that she didn't know what to do about reining her daughter in.

When they got home, Natashia finally spoke. Crying now, she turned to Cece and said, *"I hate you! I want my dad!"*

Cece only looked at her in shock as she continued saying, *"Jack has a dad, and Nancy does, too. My friends Eli and Samuel also have their dad. I don't have a dad, which is why you scold me!"*

Cece was angered more and more. There was only so much she could take. After doing everything for her daughter, this was what she got in return. Not knowing what to do, she ordered Natashia to her room and sat on the lounge chair. She dropped her head into her hands and began to truly comprehend how devastating an effect a father's absence could have on a child. She had done her best, her very best, yet here she was – clueless as to how to deal with her child, who had become so difficult and unpredictable.

It was the second time in her life after she had learned of Brad's betrayal that Cece felt the world shrinking before her eyes. She felt pained but didn't know what she could do to ease it. There must be something, she thought desperately. This time, however, she could see no glimmer of light at the end of the tunnel she had found herself in. Once more, she was on her own.

Chapter 4 – Life in the Island

That day, night fell on the island quite suddenly. Cece watched through the small closed glass of the window, as the trees were yanked this way and that by the force of the wind. The gusts were blowing at a terrible speed, and Cece felt as if the house was swaying under its pressure.

The weather was lashing out against them, and there was nothing they could do except wait and hope. Natashia was blissfully unaware of the danger. This was a vacation for her, so she ran around the house playing with Jack and Nancy. It was Cece and her sister Mary, who were worried to death of what the storm would do to their house.

"Do you think the roof would be able to stand this?" Cece asked Mary, biting her lip nervously.

"Let's hope for the best, Cece," Mary answered briskly.

They had already done the best they could to protect themselves against the storm. In the afternoon, Mary had brought over some plywood, and together, they had boarded the house with the extra wood to provide some buffering against the storm they knew would intensify with time. Mary got hold of Jack as he ran past her. Just then, there was a loud banging noise; something had hit the tin roof of the house pretty hard. The three children looked on with wide eyes and began screaming and crying. Mary tried to get the children to calm down, but they kept bawling.

"Enough!" she said loudly. *"Keep quiet, you three. Just go to your room there and sit down on the cushions. Nothing's going to happen."*

The three kids meekly followed Mary's instruction and went inside the room. Cece and Mary followed soon after, and together, the five of them remained huddled on the ground for a few minutes, listening to the sounds of the storm pounding the roof of their house.

Cece got up and twisted the knob of the old radio, trying to see if they would get any reception. Luckily, there was a signal! The children eagerly approached the small device that served as their only connection to the outside world.

The newscaster's voice came traveling on the waves: *"Mighty hurricane slams into several places on the south coast, with winds reaching the speed of over 180 miles an hour."* The news report went on to detail how the storm was unprecedented in its intensity in recent history. It also told the citizens to observe safety measures for the storm could prove to be deadly. Cece and Mary exchanged a worried glance with each other and remained quiet.

"Let's sing songs!" suggested Mary.

There was an enthusiasm in her voice that belied the anxiety that went through her on hearing the news bulletin on the radio. She got the children singing gospel songs with herself and Cece harmonizing; this was one way of keeping the children still and distracted. The dim light from the candle and the kerosene lamp cast their wavering shadows on the walls of the small house. The children sang along for a while, their attention diverted from the storm, till they finally drifted off to restless, fitful sleep.

Every time the storm howled loudly and banged against their rickety house, pounding the roof and battering the walls, one or the children would wake up screaming in terror. Cece and Mary did not sleep a wink during the night, and only tried to soothe the children who were tense even as they slept. Perhaps in their dreams, too, a dark storm raged. Sometime during the night, a gust of wind blew in through the cracks in the door and extinguished the candle and the lamp, plunging the small room in darkness. Cece and Mary groped for the matches to light it up. They couldn't sleep, no matter how much they tried. Morning took its time coming. Finally, the storm abated at dawn. As the morning sun rose limply over the eastern horizon, unable to completely break through and light up the village yet, Mary and Cece decided to head out of the house to take inventory of the damage caused by the storm during the night.

The children were still sleeping, so they breathed a sigh of relief – at least they didn't have to deal with those bundles of boundless energy yet! They really didn't want to run after the children running around in all the wreckage that they knew would greet them outside. The sight that welcomed them was much worse than they had imagined – or hoped to encounter.

Cece saw that the kitchen, which was attached to the main house but was outside the main building, was completely destroyed. Its roof had collapsed, and the meager implements they had were strewn about the sludge in the yard. Then there was the outhouse. The strong winds had entirely uprooted the old structure. This induced a new worry in Cece: where on earth were they going to go and relieve themselves when nature called? This was most certainly a bigger wreck than they had anticipated.

Cece turned to Mary with tears in her eyes, *"Mary, how am I ever going to make arrangements for repair?"*

Mary knew what was on Cece's mind. Her financial condition was poor already and to pay for such extensive rebuilding would require more than Cece could afford. She didn't know what to do at present than to console her sister.

She rubbed Cece's arm and said, *"We'll see what we can do, Cece. Don't worry about it right now, let's go take care of the children first?"* She could already hear Natasha whimpering *"Mommy? Mommy!"* through the open doorway of the house. No doubt the morning light had woken her up.

The children were all up and came outside, looking at the destruction with surprise in their eyes. The extensive damage obviously didn't register on them in the same way as it did on the adults. Cece and Mary watched as Natashia, followed by Jack and Nancy, ran hither and thither in the light drizzle that started to fall. They puttered around in the mud, dipping their feet in it, without giving a care to their clothes or appearance.

They laughed and fooled around, endlessly amused by the sludge that had given them a new playground. The debris and the twigs and branches that littered the surroundings were mere toys for them to use in their games. In the days that followed, life became more challenging for Cece, who tried to earn some extra income to fund the mending of the house. It wasn't easy as the storm had left the entire island in a shambles.

Luckily, the main building of their house had remained intact, though the roof had been damaged and leaked in some places. Natashia, however, was blissfully unaware of the dire financial strait of her mother. To her, the storm was only a hiccup in the daily routine of things. Sure, it got in the way, but she was soon able to go to her school, which was the only sign of restored normalcy that she needed.

It was only when Natashia had grown up that she realized that the storm had left a strong imprint on her memories. In adulthood, she could still recall with clarity the wailing winds, the fear it had made her feel, and the damage that she saw in the subsequent days, though at the time she wasn't particularly moved by it.

Natashia continued going to school with Jack and Nancy. The three kids had to travel for an hour by bus to get to their school. It was from that time that Natashia began to become aware of one thing: so many other children of her class had their fathers pick them up from school, but that somehow never happened with Natashia. Even Jack and Nancy had a father who would play with them and spend time with them, but there was absolutely no one for Natashia.

She didn't question Cece about it, though. She was biding her time. Natashia still hadn't made a lot of friends at school. She used to stick to Jack and Nancy even at school. They were like siblings, who were always with her no matter what. Natashia would never have realized it on her own, perhaps if the adults around her had not made her aware of the fact of their difference.

Nancy and Natashia dressed up the same way, with their hair in a braid tied neatly with colorful ribbons as they went to school in their khaki brown overall dress with a green collar and half sleeves. There was nothing different about Nancy and herself, as far as Natashia was concerned. One day when Natashia was playing outside her house, a neighbor of her aunt came to visit. She looked at Natashia and then in a voice loud enough to hear, remarked, *"This little girl looks nothing like Nancy or Jack, Mary. How are they even cousins?"* There was an obvious surprise in her words.

"Well, they are cousins. How are your kids?" Mary tried to deflect the conversation. She could see from the corner of her eyes that Natashia was listening.

"They're good. So why does your niece look so different?" the nosy woman obviously didn't want to be diverted from this line of conversation.

"Natashia is just a little different, Lily. She actually is the most intelligent child of our family! She's going on six years now, and she's already one of the best students of her class," Mary grinned widely to show how proud she was of Natashia. It was meant more for her niece than for her neighbor, of course. She didn't want Natashia to feel hurt at the woman's insensitive remarks and was trying to make up for her lack of sensitivity.

"Hmph, that's good!" Lily answered, distractedly.

She took another look at Natashia and Nancy playing and then smiled at the fairer girl and said, *"She's sure pretty, Mary. I mean your daughter Nancy. She's going to grow up to be a beauty."*

The topic of conversation shifted after that, but Natashia would forever remember the words that the woman had said and implied. She said nothing to her aunt or to her mother, but neither could she completely recover from the blow that the words had caused to her self-worth. After this one incident, Natashia started to notice how people treated Nancy and her differently. They'd always slip in a compliment or two about Nancy's prettiness, but never say a good word about Natashia's appearance. The difference in attitude would often be slight, but Natashia, being highly sensitive to the changes in tone, even at an early age, would pick up on it.

In time, Natashia became more and more aware that of being 'dark' – and also started to internalize people's opinion that it meant she was not beautiful. Unconsciously, she began to wish she were a few shades lighter, so people could say she was pretty, too. In her class, several of her classmates had the same complexion like hers, but she didn't know if they, also, felt the way that she did about her looks. This was because she was still a very isolated child and had not made a lot of friends at school. Natashia didn't say it out loud, but she was very much hurt by the fact that no one ever complimented her for her looks. Even as a child, she never expressed her vulnerability. She was a no-nonsense girl, who never backed down from a fight, so it was her nature to keep her weaknesses, supposed and real, hidden from others. So she never let anyone know how deep her insecurities about her looks ran, and how it only got worse with time. Then there was also the fact of her absent father that made her feel less valued than her fellows. It was a pity that Cece could do nothing about either.

***

It was when Natashia was six years old that Brad, her father, came to visit them again. At this time, Natashia was old enough to understand that this tall man standing before her was a significant person in her life. She could tell that by the way her mother pursed her lips and turned away from him that he wasn't a stranger, but someone her mom knew and quite possibly did not like. So it came as a surprise when Cece turned to the man and introduced him in these words: *"This is your dad, Natashia. His name is Brad."*

The man who was her father smiled at her from a safe distance. He didn't approach Natashia or try to hug her – he only smiled at her like a stranger would. Natashia registered the difference between her dad and other kids' dads, who would pick them up and laugh and hug them.

"Hello, Natashia," Brad said, smiling stiffly. He still remembered the tantrum Natashia had thrown years ago when he had come to see her. He was a little reluctant to approach her and kept to a side, closely watching her for her reaction.

Natashia chose to behave like a child would. She gingerly approached her father; this man who looked like a giant to her, and began asking questions. Brad could not keep up with her pace. She bombarded him with questions of who he was and what he did and where he lived and how come he never ever came to see or play with her if he was really her dad. Brad had no answers to most of the little girl's relentless questions. He decided to distract her with a few presents that he'd brought with him as an afterthought.

"Look, Natashia, I got you some gifts. Here, take a look," he said, pulling the shopping bag to him, and opening it wide. Inside the bag were no toys, but there were two frocks that he gave to his daughter. She looked at them and put them aside, not finding them particularly interesting to look at. Cece watched from a distance and smirked on the inside. It

was just like him to think that two dresses would make up for all his years of absence. He didn't spend much time with Natashia that evening and promised to pick her up from school the next day and take her for an ice-cream. Natashia was on cloud nine. Though she had little attachment to this man who was her father, she was really excited that for the first time in her life, she was going to have a father to show to all her class fellows, who looked at her strangely because she had never come to the school with her dad.

Cece did not try to stop Natashia from feeling happy, although based on her past experience, she did not have a very good feeling about Brad's promise. She didn't want her daughter to be disappointed by him as she was, but there was nothing she could do. The next morning, Natashia went to school with a spring in her step.

She was terribly excited and couldn't wait for the day to end, so her dad could pick her up from school in front of her entire class as he had promised. She was happy all day and even told some of her classmates that today, her dad would be there at school to take her for an ice-cream. The entire day she was restless and impatient. Finally, the last class ended, and she ran out to the school ground and was at the main gate in no time.

Time passed, and most of her classmates left the school. On their way, they stared at Natashia curiously. Natashia could read the question in their eyes, which was the same as the question in her mind: where was her dad? He had said he would be there, but he wasn't. Ten minutes passed then twenty then half an hour. It was close to forty-five minutes after school had ended, and her dad had still not shown up when Jack insisted they head home now.

Nancy and Jack were waiting with her, of course. To them, she was their little sister, and they were always there by her side to protect her. Natashia had tears in her eyes, as she finally accepted the fact that her dad won't come to pick her up like he had said. On the way home, she shed a few tears of pain at the first betrayal of her life. She was too young to be fully aware of the little betrayals that her dad had already gifted her and her mom with.

This was the first time that she'd had a taste of the terrible hurt and disappointment that her mother Cece had already suffered years ago at the hands of her dad. The next day, several of her classmates snickered, as they taunted her: *"Natashia, didn't you dad come to pick you up? Didn't you say he would come?"* With a cruelty peculiar to children, they ridiculed her and broke her heart.

"Maybe he doesn't like you either, perhaps he thinks you are ugly, too – that's why he didn't come," one girl spitefully commented. Natashia wanted to get up and pull her hair, but she didn't. She knew her mother would be very upset if the school told her Natashia had hurt her class fellow. She remained stone-faced all day and did not cry though she badly wanted to. In her heart grew the feeling of being ashamed of herself, of her dad – she was a child and didn't know any other way of dealing with the setback Brad had given her.

***

Days passed then months, and still, Natashia didn't forget the actions of her dad, who didn't show up at all after that first day. Secretly, she kept waiting for him to come to the house and say sorry for not coming to pick her up like he'd said. After all, that's how things were supposed to work. When you did something wrong – like not keeping your promise – you had to apologize for it. In her heart, she was all prepared to be mad at her dad, only to forgive him after a while if he acted sorry enough. Things never came to that, however, as Brad left the island some days later without ever coming to see Natashia again.

Cece was furious at his actions and knew that he must have felt no remorse at doing what he had done to his daughter. She didn't say anything to Natashia though, as she didn't want her to harbor too many negative feelings against the man who was, after all, her father. Natashia spent the time with her cousins and maternal family like she always did. They were the only family she knew and was pretty close to them. She spent the next summer vacations on the island beaches as she always did. It was Cece and her sister's ritual to take the children to the beach during the summers, so they could run around and climb trees to their hearts' fill. Taking those days off was a way for them to unwind and spend some bonding time together.

It was during this summer before she turned seven years old that Natashia confronted her fear of the ocean. As always, they were at the beach when one of her cousins, who was about nine or ten at this time, pulled her arm and began dragging her to the sea. Though she had lived all her life on the island, Natashia was scared of water. She yelled and screamed loudly to get her cousin to let go of her.

"I just want you to swim! It's easy!" insisted her cousin, as Natashia screamed at the top of her lungs.

She was small and was easily dragged by the older girl to the water, where she splashed helplessly in the water, tears running down her face. Natashia was gasping for breath when another older cousin rescued her. The girl who had dragged her to the sea got the scolding of her life for forcing Natashia to enter the sea when she didn't want to. That was that of this incident.

The summers were spent in carefree indulgence, the likes of which are particular only to childhood. Natashia later recalled how they would have mango eating competitions during the summers at the beach. They would all gorge on mangoes, which would often end with them contracting diarrhea. This never stopped them from overeating, though; to them, this was a summer game which they wanted to win at all costs.

Natashia also learned to make clay dolls with Nancy during this time. They would make dolls out of the mud on the beach, and let them dry and harden in the sun. The dolls would come out looking smooth and swarthy, and just the right shape. Natashia was pleased to see that the dolls they made looked more like her than the other dolls sold in the shops on the island that were always a whole lot fair than she was. It was well after summer ended that Natashia heard from her dad again. This time he didn't come to visit her at her house; he sent her a letter all the way from England instead. This was the first time that she had received a letter in her life. Natashia straightaway read the entire letter from start to end – she was still unconsciously hoping to receive the apology for what he had done last year. However, the letter said no such thing. There was no mention of his promise of picking her up from school, let alone of being sorry about breaking that promise.

The letter contained only words, which Natashia, even at her young age, found hard to believe. There were greetings and general things, nothing of much importance. She read the letter again – it perfunctorily said 'I love you,' but Natashia knew enough not to believe the words. She was so mad and disappointed at the letter that she wanted to burn it or throw it in the trash can or just to send it back to him.

She did none of those things; however, and hid the letter underneath her mattress, so no one else could read it. It was a few days after this that Natashia's great uncle visited the island. This was another strange man who suddenly visited her house one day. This man was nothing like her dad, however. Where her dad was young and handsome, this man was old and hairy with gold teeth, which showed every time he smiled widely. Natashia watched him, fascinated, as he talked about his life in America. This great uncle of Natashia had left the island when Cece was younger than she was now. This fact made Natashia's eyes pop in disbelief. She couldn't ever imagine a time when her mom was a little baby! So this uncle had left for America where he had lived for 31 long years. He'd come back only now – and without any gifts, Natashia noted, crinkling her nose in displeasure. It just went plain against the island rules to visit your relatives empty-handed after years and years abroad.

"Maybe he's forgotten how things work on the island, as he's lived away for so long," Nancy had whispered in her ear, giggling. Natashia agreed with that analysis. This great uncle stayed on the island for three whole weeks during which he became one of Natashia's favorite people ever. He would talk to Natashia often and in English-based Creole, a language she had learned from her great grandma Sasa.

He used to tell her jokes and stories about his wealth in America. He would just make her laugh. The best thing was that he was dark in appearance, just like Natashia. So spending time with him, Natashia felt like she fit right in. There was none of that sense of not belonging or of being inferior that she had lately started feeling around people, who were fairer than her in complexion. And he also gave Natashia pennies to buy candies so that obviously made Natashia like him more and more! Natashia didn't realize it then and nor did Cece, but growing up in such an environment where she was devalued because of her skin color was really damaging the little girl's self-image.

Though Natashia was an overachiever in class and had an outstanding academic record, she didn't garner any of the praises that she should have for her brilliance. Slowly but surely, her self-esteem was being targeted. It would only become apparent later how much damage people's careless words and discriminating attitude did to the little girl, who was her mother's whole world.

Chapter 5 – Bullying

"Hey, Mrs. Team!"

Natashia turned around at the words that seemed to be directed at her. It was early morning, and she had just arrived at school. There was still time before classes would begin. Her ponytail of dark, spring-like hair bounced in the air, as she turned her face this way and that, trying to locate the speaker of those words. It always took Cece a good time to tie Natashia's rebellious tight curls.

'Her hair just has a mind of its own, just like her!' Cece always thought. Natashia finally spotted the giggling girls. There were three of them – light-skinned, it immediately registered on Natashia, and a lot taller than she was – who were now pointing at her and whispering in each other's ears.

Natashia watched them under furrowed brows. She knew for a fact it was bad manners to point your finger at someone and whisper about them, and especially when they could see you! She knew because her mommy had told her so. Never one to back down, she charged toward them, her small hands on her hips. She was going to be eight years old soon but had more pluck than kids twice her age. Still, incidents of bullying occurred at an almost daily basis at the school. She decided to confront the giggling girls, who were also whispering and pointing to her direction.

Approaching them, she first decided to confirm, *"Was it you who just called me Mrs. Team?"*

The one who appeared to be the leader of the pack said, *"Yeah, because you are! Mrs. Team, Mrs. Team!"* The other two girls joined in the chorus.

The three of them surrounded Natashia and got too close to her face, singing the words as if they were a nursery rhyme, only they were angry and hateful like no nursery poem could be. Natashia was bewildered by the sudden onslaught. She lost her usual confidence in the face of such hostility, which she had done nothing to invite.

Her hands began to shake, and tears welled up in her eyes. She started to back away, so she could break out of the circle they had formed around her. Just then, a teacher appeared at the far edge of the school ground. One of the girls saw her and told the other two. The three of them stopped what they were doing immediately and ran inside the school building. Natashia watched them run and stared in the direction they had vanished, long after they had disappeared from sight. She suddenly felt drained of all energy, like she would faint and fall down to the ground. When the school bell rang, she picked up the bag, which had dropped to the ground without her even realizing sometime during this episode of humiliation. Her new Mr. Team bag, which her mom had bought to her as a present just last weekend and which she had brought to school for the first time today, was caked with dust.

One of the girls had stepped on it as she had run, and there was a footprint of her shoes on it. Natashia didn't care. She didn't dust the bag off and only dragged it with her as she walked to the class. Quietly, with her eyes gone blank, she took her seat. She took out the required books and her notebook automatically. She didn't know, but this was only the start of the long period of bullying that she was to face at the hands of her schoolfellows.

***

Cece noticed that for some days now, Natashia had begun to dislike going to school. It wasn't that she'd said such a thing out loud or that she cried or faked illness in the mornings to get out of attending school. But she just didn't seem as excited for school as she always used to before. Natashia was a good student. She loved learning, and she loved being at school in general, unlike most kids. She was doing exceptionally well in her class, and her teachers still loved her. So her recent disinterest worried Cece. One night, she decided to ask Natashia directly.

She said, *"Don't you like school anymore?"*

Natashia looked at her with wide eyes quietly for a moment before answering, *"Why are you saying that, Mommy?"*

Cece said, *"Just asking. You used to love going to school, but now you are always so lazy in the mornings. You also told me you don't want to take your new bag to school when you had begged me to get it for weeks."*

"Yeah, but you still force me to take it to school," Natashia complained.

"I threw away your old bag, Natashia! You have no other bag than this one. Remember you loved it so much before?" Cece protested.

"Well, I don't love it anymore," Natashia said as she wrapped her arms around her stomach defensively.

"But why?"

"I don't want to tell you," Natashia answered moodily.

"Then who will you tell?" Cece demanded.

"Not you. You won't get it!"

Cece saw Natashia's hurt in her eyes. She softened her voice and said, *"Honey, what's the matter? You can tell me. I promise I will listen and understand."*

Tears gathered in Natashia's eyes and fell down her face. Cece reached out to wipe them and pulled Natashia into her lap. Between hiccups, her daughter said, *"The...the...mean girls...girls say mean things to me. The...they said...said I was 'Mrs. Team'."* *"Mrs. What?"* Cece demanded.

"Mrs. Team!" Natashia repeated.

"Which girls are these?" Cece asked next.

"They're three sisters. They called me that first, and now they've got half the school calling me the same name. I don't like it. I hate it. This is why I didn't want to take the bag with me," Natashia explained.

"I see," Cece said, thinking for a moment. Then she came up with a solution she thought was really good.

Turning to Natashia, she said, *"Honey, don't pay them no mind. If you ignore them, they will get bored and leave you alone. Just focus on your studies. If you come in top of your class, all of them will know how smart you are. They will think twice about bothering you again!"*

Natashia nodded, taking her mom's advice with the complete trust peculiar to children.

Cece didn't realize that things didn't work like this anymore – or that they never had. Her intelligence was just one more thing for the bullies to target. If this is how things worked, then those kids would never have bullied Natashia in the first place because she always excelled in her studies. She also continued to receive golden stars for her excellent performance. If anything, this made the three girls and others jealous; as a result, they became more and more brutal with time.

***

Summer came, and it was a massive relief to Natashia who only wanted to be away from school and the bullies who never left her alone. She hoped fervently that next year, those sisters will have left her class or better yet, the school. With this hope in her heart, she began her summer break with optimism. This time, instead of spending the summer with her maternal family like she usually did, she was visiting her father's family. It was Cece's idea because she liked her paternal grandparents and wanted Natashia to have strong ties with them. The two families were as different as night and day. Natashia's paternal grandmother's house was in a village to the south of the island. Natashia didn't mind going there, as she had a good friendship with one of her cousins Terry. She was quite excited to see her!

Summer, with her maternal family, meant long months at the beach. It meant eating tropical food until she got sick on them. Natashia, just like her cousins, always ate too much of it. The guava gave them constipation, and the mangoes gave them diarrhea, but nothing could stop them. Then, during summers, they also collected almonds.

Natashia had learned the subtle art of breaking almond shells delicately by putting them on a stone, tilting them at a specific angle and then hitting the shell gently, so it broke open instead of getting smashed. The cousins also held almond breaking competitions; whoever broke open the most shells and collected the most whole almonds in the jars would win. Then, they also roasted chicken on a pit at the beach. They also ate sweet potatoes and breadfruit.

Sometimes, they would make breadfruit balls, which Natashia didn't like at all. Spending time at her paternal grandmother's house was a different kind of fun altogether. Their family was really strict and had rules, which they were required to follow. Their house was small, and the kitchen was outside, but Natashia didn't mind such things at all. Living with her father's family over the summers introduced Natashia to a whole new way of life. She saw that her aunts were all nurses, and her uncles were in business.

Viewing such different people opened up a new world for Natashia. So English-based Creole was a no-no in this family. None of her aunts and uncles or cousins used that language at home. Though her grandmother talked to her husband and neighbors in English based Creole, when talking to her children and grandchildren, she only spoke in English.

When she got there, her grandmother gave her a big hug and kiss. At the same time, she said to Natashia, *"Now you behave like a proper young lady, Natashia. You're growing up! Soon you'll be eight, so don't go around dipping in the sea, wearing your panties only. I would like to have a modest granddaughter, please."*

Even if she hadn't said it, it was the unspoken rule for the girls on the island that they could go swimming in the sea in only their panties till age seven, but after that, they were required to wear a top or a swimwear. Natashia nodded respectfully, just like Cece had taught her. She had a good time eating and playing with her cousin Terry who was her age. The two of them ran around outside so much that they were exhausted and fell asleep on the sofa instead of in their bed.

The next morning, Natashia got ready after breakfast to help out at her grandmother's grocery shop, which was right next to their house. She sold candies and juicy tamarind balls, among other things, but these were the two items that Natashia and Terry loved the most. She got behind the counter, which was so high that it completely covered her.

Then, she brought a professional frown on her face, copying her grandma as best as she could. A few customers came and bought different treats. Her grandma gave her the money to count before she put it in the little box that she hid beneath the counter. It wasn't long before the sight of those treats made Natashia's mouth water. She and Terry looked at each other – both recognized the thought in the other's mind.

Next, both of them looked at their grandma, who was busy ridding the counter of some invisible dust by rubbing a cloth hard over it. The fact of grandma's distraction confirmed, the two of them looked slyly at each other and then at the tamarind balls. Then quiet as a mouse, Natashia put her hand inside the open jar and took as many of those balls out as she could. Terry followed her and did the same.

It was a scary but also an extremely exciting game for them to stuff the balls in their mouth and swallow it down every time their grandma turned away. The sour-sweetness melted in their mouths and eating so much of it so fast brought tears to their eyes, but they didn't care. It was only later when their grandma asked them to pay for their stealing by doing household chores that they realized she had known what they were up to all along.

Natashia, surprised, couldn't help but ask, *"But how did you know, grandma?"*

The old woman smiled and answered, *"It's because I have eyes in the back of my head."*

***

At her grandmother's place, Natashia also met her half-siblings for the first time. She, who had always thought she was an only child, found out that her father had several children before her, all of them from different women. When she grew up, she realized her father was a bona fide womanizer, and for him, her mother Cece was nothing but one in a long string of women. At present, however, she was astonished to see that she had five older brothers. She met them at her grandma's because they, too, visited her from time to time. One of them had even grown up at her grandma's place because she had taken him in when he was born. Usually, when they came over during summers, they spent their time helping around in the garden – or so her grandmother said.

Natashia was a little pleased to have brothers, but she didn't get a chance to establish friendships with any of them. To her disappointment, none of her half-brothers looked like her. They looked like her dad, being as tall and light-skinned as him. None of them wanted anything to do with their father, however, as he had demonstrated as little interest in their wellbeing, emotional or financial, as he had in Natashia's. She didn't grow close to any of her brothers who, on their part, never treated her like a sister. The worst one was Lawrence.

He was a few years older than her, yet he seemed to have formed a grudge against her for a reason Natashia couldn't understand. One day, when Natashia was inside the house helping out, along with Terry, he did the absolute worst. He had just come from outside, perhaps taking a break from running wild.

Natashia had heard her grandmother mutter several times that Lawrence seemed to be taking right after his dad. So Natashia never had a good impression of him anyway. He observed Natashia going from room to room, cleaning up after the mess he had taken part in creating. As she ignored him and laughed with Terry, he addressed no one in particular and loudly said, *"You know what?"*

Natashia, her grandma, and Terry, as well as another aunt who was in the house at the time, all turned to look at him since no one knew who he was talking to. Pleased to have everybody's attention, he smirked and said, *"I never expected to have a sister who'd be so dark!"*

And then added, *"She's too black to be my sister!"*

In the silence that followed, Natashia could hear her heart beating fast. She was stunned to the point of speechlessness. No one else said anything either, perhaps because they'd never expected Lawrence to say such a thing. Natashia felt defenseless as if she had no one in the world. Her mother was far away. Jack and Nancy, who always protected her from the bullies, were also not there.

The truth was, Natashia had never been subjected to such mistreatment at home. Home had always been a safe place for her, where she was well-guarded from all the hate that other people directed at her. She had thought her grandma's place would be the same safe haven for her – apparently, it wasn't, not with someone like Lawrence around.

Just then, her grandma yelled, *"Boy, what are you saying? Quit talking or I will make you!"*

The snicker disappeared from Lawrence's face.

Their grandma looked furious. He didn't stay in the house then and walked out. Natashia breathed a sigh of relief and turned to her grandma with gratitude in her eyes. Her grandma only smiled and hugged her close. Once again, Natashia felt protected and safe.

***

That summer ended, and school resumed. Time had passed, but the bullying still remained the same. It was the same relentless persecution for Natashia. The three girls were still in her class and were as merciless and unthinkingly cruel as ever before. During the year that had passed, they had targeted several areas of Natashia's life to taunt and mock her.

Foremost among those, of course, was her skin color. When she was younger, Natashia had only understood that her complexion made her stand out and never impressed the island people, who only loved whiteness. It was only at the hands of her class fellows that she learned the full extent of the bias, which almost resembled hate against black skin.

"Hey darkie!" a young boy had called Natashia once.

Natashia had flushed with humiliation and anger that one time. Her ears had turned hot, and her vision had become blurry. By this time, Natashia had begun to hate her skin with an intensity she couldn't fathom at her age. Lawrence's words, along with other people's behavior, had stuck to her. She wished to rub soap on herself so hard that it would peel the skin right off – perhaps then, white skin would emerge from underneath. Yet she knew that wouldn't happen.

As more time passed, she began to hate everything that was black in color, like she loathed her own skin. Once, when the road near her home was being paved, she had broken off a piece of tar and put it against her hand to compare. She wanted to see if she really was as dark as that like some kids had told her. Even though it actually wasn't, to her eyes, her skin did appear as dark as tar. Other people's views of her had distorted her self-image to the point that she couldn't see things clearly. Every time she saw a crow, she turned her face away in disgust and told herself,

'I must look as ugly to others, as this crow does to me. It's because of the blackness.'

Another time, a black cat had come sauntering inside their home. Though Natashia had always loved cats, she hated the look of this one. She had picked up her shoe and thrown it at the scrawny animal, missing it, but scaring it badly so that it ran outside. She didn't realize that she had internalized the hate that people showed toward her color. She now believed what they believed. She was holding her self-hate like a piece of jagged glass against her skin, maiming herself daily. The only difference was that no one saw the blood, and no one saw the scars because there was no visible evidence of this injury.

Such incidents of name calling now happened with so much regularity at school that Natashia had started to take them in stride. This didn't mean that they didn't affect her anymore. She didn't think there would come a time when such words wouldn't hurt her. However, she had learned her own ways to cope with it.

Unfortunately, there was no one to tell her that those ways were only a temporary escape, and additionally, were quite unhealthy. What she did was that she began to hide from people. The girl who'd had a natural confidence now retreated into her shell and started to avoid most of her peers, every time that she could.

This morning, as Natashia walked down the school hallway, almost clinging to the wall as had become her habit, she silently prayed in her heart for the three vicious girls to be absent. She made this little prayer every day, but most of the time, it went unanswered. This was just like her prayers to miraculously become fair-skinned remained unanswered, though she had been making that prayer for a whole year now. As soon as she got to the door of the classroom, however, she spotted their long curly hair and white faces.

They turned to look at her and then laughed before squeaking, *"Mrs. T!"* They, of course, made sure to keep their voices loud enough so that everyone heard. How she wished Jack and Nancy were in the same grade as her! They were the ones who kept the bullies away. Natashia felt so safe every time they came to collect her when she was late for the school bus because they were stronger and bigger than she was.

Still following her mother's advice, Natashia pretended indifference and sat beside her friend, who was as dark-skinned as she was. Though Natashia wasn't aware of it, for some time now, she had started to gravitate toward the kids who looked like her. She had only friends that weren't light-skinned. Her friend Rita turned and smiled at her before commenting, *"The Nasties got here too early today. I was waiting for you for very long! Their voices just hurt my ears sometimes!"*

Natashia giggled at this, feeling inordinately happy at Rita's observation, which she wholeheartedly agreed with. The first half of the day passed without incident, but as soon as it was lunchtime, the inevitable happened. Natashia usually waited till the last of the students had left the classroom, so she could leave at the same time as the teacher

– this was her way to cope with the threats of being beaten up that the three girls had recently started issuing. Today, however, Natashia forgot to take the usual precautions. Her mind elsewhere, she walked out of the class with the other kids. It was a minute later that someone pushed her aggressively into the wall. Natashia slammed hard against the wall and then bounced off, falling to the ground. She was the smartest in her class, and she was also the smallest. Her elbow was scraped badly, and her knees also hurt. Rita came quickly to help her get up on her feet, but when the two of them looked around, they didn't see the three bullies.

"I know it was them," Natashia said, wiping away her tears.

"I know that too! Gosh, I hate those three girls. I am so mad at them, I could punch them all the way to the beach!" Rita replied.

Natashia laughed at the image that appeared in her head. Then, on Rita's and some other friends' insistence, she decided to finally report the behavior of the three girls to her teacher, who later reported it to the headmistress. She went to the headmistress's office, and after being let in, showed her skinned elbows and knees to her.

The old woman peered at her and the injuries from underneath her glasses. When the three girls entered the room, their faces betrayed their panic. But they quickly recovered from it because they had come armed with a plan: they outright rejected pushing Natashia.

"We didn't do it," said the first girl.

The headmistress turned to Natashia and asked, *"Did you see her, or any of them do it?"*

Natashia hadn't, and so she shook her head no.

The headmistress stared at Natashia and asked, *"Well then, did anyone else see them do it? Any of your class fellows?"*

"I don't know, the hallway was crowded. So many kids were there. You can ask them," Natashia truthfully answered.

It was then that one of the girls spoke up, *"She bullies us!"*

Natashia was so dumbfounded, she actually stared at the girl with her mouth open. Before she could say a word, the other two also jumped in and pretty quickly, the three of them had concocted an entire tale for the headmistress that ended with, *"...and she calls us 'pigs' sometimes, and it's so hurtful, but we never said anything to the teacher because we didn't want to cause any trouble!"*

Natashia would have laughed, so impossible was the story that the three had come up with. However, the headmistress's next words killed the laughter that was bubbling in her throat. With a stern expression on her face, she looked down at Natashia and declared her disappointment, *"I did not expect this from you, Natashia. You are our brightest student. Now, apologize to them."*

"What?" Natashia said.

"Say you're sorry and we'll close this chapter."

Natashia was heartbroken. The headmistress had believed them, instead of her. She just wanted to get out of the office as soon as possible, so turning to the three girls, she said 'sorry' and then ran out of the room. This incident was forever engrained in her memory; no matter how hard she tried, she could not scrape it out.

Chapter 6 – The Visit

Brad was going to visit the island again. Ever since Cece had learned the news through his mother, she had felt anxious. The feeling grew as the day of his arrival got closer. It felt to her as if her heart was being squeezed in a tight fist.

It wasn't that she still loved him – there was no way she could ever feel that way about a man, who had deceived her and then abandoned his daughter – but that she didn't want to have to struggle with those old feelings of resentment and anger that resurfaced at the sight of him.

"His presence will just disturb the stability that I have worked so hard to achieve," Cece confided in her sister Mary.

Mary, while watching Natashia play with Jack and Nancy, nodded, *"It will especially upset Natashia. Do you remember what he did the last time?"*

"How can I forget?" Cece said, her face flushed in anger at the old memory. She could never forget her daughter's distraught reaction when Brad had failed to keep his word and pick her up from school. Mary turned to her sister and put her hand on her arm.

"Are you worried he's going to do something like that again?"

"I am not worried, Mary, because I know that he will. It will be something else this time, but I am sure he'll either humiliate me or hurt Natashia," Cece said, chewing her words. *"The truth is that Natashia is older than before now. I know when he does something to hurt her, I won't be able to explain it to her the reason 'why'."*

"You won't," Mary agreed. She knew how smart and sensitive her niece really was. There was no way that her father's cruel indifference hadn't registered on her yet. His up and coming visit will only compound the pain of her father's absence for Natashia. However, Mary didn't share these thoughts with Cece, knowing her sister already had a lot on her plate to deal with.

"So my daughter will grow up with feelings of abandonment," Cece said, looking to Mary for comfort.

"These are not things that you can help, Cece," Mary said. *"If he is hell-bent on making his own daughter hate him, then what can you do about it?"*

"I don't want to do anything about it. I don't care that he is hated by his own daughter. What I care about is how those

feelings will hurt my daughter. It will tear her up inside in the long run to have those negative feelings about her father," Cece said.

Mary sighed deeply, rubbing Cece's back to relax her. She wished it were that easy to soothe away her sister's very legitimate worries, but she knew she was helpless to make that happen.

***

It was summer break again. Natashia was eight years old now, and again, she was going to visit her grandmother's place. This time, though, she wasn't there to spend the entire summer but to see her father, Brad. Her father had insisted that Cece bring Natashia to his mother's place to see him.

Cece had tried to get him into visiting her house and be done with the visit, but he hadn't budged. He'd referred to the last two times he had come to her place to see Natashia and was adamant that this time Cece brings Natashia to his mother's house. He had said he'd feel more freedom to interact with her outside of the watchful gaze of Cece's family. However, Cece knew he only wanted to be on familiar turf, as that might give him an advantage. She knew Brad enough to catch on his way of thinking about things.

So reluctantly, she had come here to his mother's house. Natashia was already familiar with the place, so she bounced around happily with her cousin Terry. Cece, on her part, felt out of place. She decided she would just leave before Brad arrived. Though Brad's mother was as kind as she had always been to Cece, she couldn't stop feeling wrong about being here, much like she would feel if she had put her right slipper on her left foot and the left one on her right foot.

She sat on the wooden chair around the kitchen table awkwardly, waiting for Brad's mother to say goodbye, so she could leave. She wanted to leave before Brad arrived, not wanting to be found waiting like a servant on call. She could just imagine the satisfaction Brad would get out of the sight of her in his mother's house.

Cece wrapped her arms around herself, as Brad's mother sat down opposite her. She smiled feebly as the old woman began, *"I know this is hard for you, Cece."*

Cece nodded and said, *"He's coming with his wife and kids. I don't want to be here because I don't belong here. Of course, for Natashia it's fine because it's her grandmother's house."*

"Oh, you leave before he arrives. We can't let him have his fun," the old woman remarked with a good bit of sarcasm in her voice.

When Cece looked up at her surprised, she said, *"What are you looking at me for, girl? I know my son!"*

Huffing, she continued, *"My son is no innocent lamb. Never has been. I bet he'd get pleasure out of watching you squirm. He hates your guts, by the way."*

Cece had known Brad's parents liked her and had never gotten over how Brad had deceived her though he had actually done the same to several other women – with his several sons as proof. For some reason, his parents had taken a liking to Cece. Even now, after years of their son's betrayal, they supported Cece.

Taking her time to absorb Brad's mother's outburst against her son, she cleared her throat and said, *"Are his other children here?"*

"Yeah, they are. Where are they supposed to go? They are older and boys, so they keep visiting us. One lives here with us," the older woman said.

"Are they happy about Brad visiting? I don't know if Natashia is," Cece ventured.

"Happy?" scoffed the older woman. *"They don't like their father just like you don't like him, girl. Brad has never given them the time of day, so why would they ever want to see him?"*

"He never supported them either?" Cece asked, though she didn't quite understand why this should have come off as a surprise to her.

Brad's mother said, *"Brad has never been one for responsibilities. Let's see how he takes care of his brand new family, though. Not too much time left till I can see him with my own two eyes."*

As Cece stood up, the old woman wrapped her in a comforting hug. As she left the house, instructing Natashia to remind Brad to drop her off before too late in the night, Cece felt less alone than she did when she had arrived here that morning.

***

Brad reached his mother's house a good two hours late than the time he had given. Natashia didn't notice that he was late, however, as she was too busy playing around with Terry. When Brad arrived finally, she scrambled into the small hall of the house on her grandmother's instructions.

She stood up with her back straight and her eyes staring straight ahead, again on her grandmother's instructions. She felt as if she had done something wrong and was waiting for punishment. The voice of a little girl giggling made Natashia forget all her grandmother's orders, and she craned her neck to look outside the open door of the house. 'Who is she?' Natashia asked herself, confused, as she saw a young girl, around the same age as her, walk inside the door of the house, clutching a woman's hand.

Natashia eyes traveled all the way up from her bright red shoes to the flowery dress she had on to her pale face. She was as fair as a white girl. She had gold earrings in her ears, as Natashia saw when she bobbed her head here and there, and a gold chain around her neck. She knew this jewelry was supposed to be expensive because she remembered the white woman from her childhood – the one who'd lived in the house her mother had worked and who had given her cookies every day – used to wear it.

Her father followed the woman and the little girl. He towered over the two of them and smiled his usual charming smile, showing almost all his teeth. Natashia saw that he was holding the hand of a boy, who seemed a few years younger than the girl. The boy was brown-skinned but nowhere near as dark as Natashia, who noticed this detail at first sight. By this time, Natashia had become accustomed to immediately observing people's skin color before she noticed any other physical characteristic. She didn't do it consciously, but people's complexion was the first trait that registered in her mind. Two more children completed this happy family – both boys, a four-year-old in the arms of her father, and a baby cradled protectively by the woman.

Natashia didn't say a word, but only watched quietly as her father ignored her and spoke to his mother, introducing the woman as his wife and the four kids as his children. Now that Natashia saw her clearly, the woman who was her father's wife was undoubtedly nowhere as pretty as her own mother.

But she was wearing better clothes and was covered all over in trinkets, from her ears to her nose to her wrists to her ankles. This confirmed it to Natashia that her father and his family were a lot richer than she and her mother was. Confused by the implications of the thought, she stared absentmindedly when Brad finally approached her and said hello. He had to wave his hand in front of her a few times before she noticed him. Then politely, just like her mother and grandmother had instructed, she said, *"Hello. How are you?"*

Her father gave the now-familiar big smile that didn't reach his eyes. He shook Natashia's hand, foregoing the hug she was expecting, and said, *"I am well. And how are you?"*

Natashia opened her mouth to answer him, but he turned away before she could get out the appropriate words. He pulled the light-skinned girl who was also his daughter to him and said to Natashia, *"This is Uma, my daughter. She is your half-sister. And there here are Dylan, Matthew, and Jimmy; your half-brothers."*

The girl called Uma stared at Natashia's face and then wrinkled her nose before reluctantly reaching out her hand toward Natashia, who grabbed the hand and shook it just as half-heartedly as her and said, *"Hi, I am Natashia."*

Uma nodded and then sidled away toward her mother, who was busy gesturing wildly with her hands, explaining the ride to the island to Brad's mom. Natashia glanced at her grandmother's face and saw the barely concealed expression of boredom there. Suppressing her smile at that, she nudged Terry with her elbow and began to giggle.

The rest of the time passed quickly enough for Natashia, who had Terry to keep her company. Uma and her younger brother Jimmy stuck to each other and didn't speak to Natashia again. Her dad sat down on the couch and answered his mother's questions with irritated expressions on his face that he did little to conceal. Natashia thought Uma was perhaps too shy to talk to her. Another dark thought appeared in her head: that Uma didn't want to speak to her because she was too dark. Then deciding to think about it later, she whiled the rest of the time playing hopscotch with Terry, who remained by her side till the sunset.

It was around 10 in the night that Brad unenthusiastically got on his feet to drop Natashia back to her house. He practically dragged his feet to the door of the house, holding Natashia's hand in a loose grip. Before Natashia left, her dad's wife gave her a shopping bag – Natashia saw that there were a dress and a pair of shoes inside – which she took with a polite 'thank you', just as her mother had taught her. When they got to her mother's house, Natashia saw that the lights were still on. She felt glad to be home, away from the strange eyes of her father's wife and children.

Natashia's mind was in a tumultuous state. She couldn't stop wondering why her father's wife and four kids were so rich, and why she and her mother weren't. She couldn't stop questioning why he lived with them and not with her and her mother. She had noticed that none of her half-brothers had been particularly happy to see their father. She was slowly starting to understand the life of deprivation granted to her by her father was what she had in common with her half-brothers. As for the four children, they had lived a sheltered life and seemed to have it all.

Natashia saw her mother's tensed face when she greeted Brad. She asked Natashia to say 'thank you' and 'goodnight' to her father and then told her to go inside, change, and get into bed. Natashia did as she was asked. Cece turned to look at Brad waiting for him to leave, so she could bang the door shut behind him. After dawdling for a few minutes, he walked out the door, and Cece went to Natashia to listen to her account of the day. Natashia, who had a vivid imagination, described her father's wife and four children to Cece in minute detail. Listening about their appearance and attitude, Cece felt a pang inside her heart. 'So Brad has decked his wife and daughter in gold, but he has nothing to give to his other daughter,' Cece thought, nodding absentmindedly at Natashia as she finished relating the day's activity to her. It was only after Natashia had gone to sleep that Cece allowed herself to cry. The disparity between Natashia and Brad's other children was too much for her to bear. However, she knew she could do nothing about it. If she had to struggle for her daughter, then she would. She didn't need a Brad to make life easier for her.

***

The weeks of her father's stay on the island passed swiftly. He wasn't here on a long vacation; if anything, he had seemed ready to leave as soon as he'd arrived. Natashia barely saw him two or three more times. The little time she spent with him left little mark on Natashia's memory. Soon, it was time for him to go. He came to say goodbye to Natashia at her place.

Natashia said bye to him, as she would to a casual visitor. She felt none of the attachment a child feels with her father. She was secretly relieved to see him leave because now she wouldn't have to see her half-siblings again. After Natashia said goodbye to Brad and went inside her room, Cece walked Brad to the door. Just as she was ready to close the door on him, he turned back and took an envelope from the inside pocket of his jacket and handed it to Cece. She instinctively reached out and grabbed the envelope. Then, regretting her action immediately, but seeing no way to hand it back to him while still keeping face, she asked tersely, *"What's this?"*

"See for yourself," Brad replied infuriatingly.

Cece could already tell what the contents might be, but couldn't believe it until she ripped open envelope and saw them for herself. There were coins inside the envelope – loose change. Brad cleared his throat and said, *"This is to help you with Natashia's care. I thought I would pitch in."*

Cece couldn't believe her eyes or her ears. Pitch in? She shook her head in disbelief, the sour taste of resentment and humiliation in her mouth. As Brad retreated, she slammed the door behind him. As she wiped away the tears that fell from her eyes, she told herself she shouldn't have been surprised.

He had no use for those coins and could spare them, so he had handed them over to Cece. He had never been a father to Natashia and never will be. Even so, this was a new low, even for him. Bitterly, Cece put the money away in a tin box. Despite hating Brad for doing this, she knew she could use the money for taking care of some impending chores.

***

After what seemed like ages of scrimping and saving up, Cece was able to move with Natashia into a somewhat bigger house with better facilities. This house came with electricity and water and was closer to the main road. Natashia was ecstatic to move into a new house, which seemed as shiny as a penny to her. She jumped around the entire first week, exploring the residence, even though it wasn't as big as all that.

The water supply in this new house wasn't regular, and sometimes, Natashia and Cece had to fill up two-liter water bottles and carry them to the house. They had to travel as long as two miles on foot for this. Jack and Nancy came over to visit, and they did this chore with Natashia, leaving Cece free to take care of other tasks.

Natashia loved this new but temporary arrangement, not because she particularly liked to carry those heavy water bottles, but because she liked her new companions more than she did her mother. The only reason for that was her mother kept up a continuous stream of objections all through the walk. Cece would tell Natashia, *"Don't wrap your arms around the bottle, Natashia! It's not a baby for you to carry* it like this!" or "Look at those other girls carrying the bottle on their heads. That is the safe way."

Natashia, being her stubborn self, always ignored those instructions. She said she'd carry it in her hands or her head another time, but that another time never arrived. It was on one of these trips with Jack and Nancy that her mother's worst predictions came true. Natashia was walking up the road, talking to her cousins, and not paying attention to where she was going. She tripped on a rock and fell. The glass bottle which she was carrying in her embrace broke. The shards of glass pierced through Natashia's skin. She screamed from the pain that shot through her body. Her pale blue dress was bloodied and torn. Jack ran to the house and called Cece, who came running down the street to her daughter.

Cece almost panicked at the sight of her little daughter down on the road, covered in blood. Natashia wasn't crying, though. This reassured Cece somewhat, who was, once more, taken aback by her young daughter's show of resilience. She carried Natashia back to the house. Once there, she, along with Jack and Nancy, picked out the small and big pieces of glass from Natashia's dress and skin. Cece breathed a sigh of relief to see that the injury wasn't severe and did not need stitches. Giving Natashia some time to recover from shock, Cece delivered a blistering scolding to Natashia and forbade her to carry the bottle like that ever again. For the first time, Natashia nodded her head quietly and agreed to carry the bottle in her hand like her mother had always asked her to.

Chapter 7 – Education

"He's coming to visit again?" Natashia asked with wide eyes. She couldn't wrap her head around the fact that Brad, her father, who had barely visited the island for the eight or nine years of her life, was going to be back so soon. She recalled the last summer he had been here with his wife and four kids. Her expression soured as it occurred to her that his family might visit with him, too, just like the last time.

"Yes, but this time he is coming alone," Cece answered, as though reading her mind. Then she added, *"He is going to pick you up from school."*

"Why?"

"He says he wants to take you out to lunch and then to a drive. Won't that be fun?" Cece said with a forced smile.

"I don't know," Natashia answered moodily, then wandered away, already thinking of what she might say to her dad who was still very much a stranger to her.

The next Monday, as soon as school ended, she walked out the gates to see her dad waiting by his car. He was dressed so oddly that Natashia stopped in her tracks and surreptitiously looked here and there to see if other kids had seen him and were laughing at him for his bizarre appearance. He wore cowboy boots and a long-sleeved shirt and tight jeans. It might not have been as crazy if it wasn't the middle of summer on the island with the weather humid and sweltering. Natashia walked to him quickly, and after a short greeting, hopped into the front seat of his car. He drove fast without speaking and stopped at a nearby restaurant, which Natashia had not been to before.

Natashia took a seat opposite to him on the table and tapped her fingers on the table, as her father looked at her with a smile that, once again, did not reach his eyes. She took care to keep her elbows off the top of the table because those were good manners like her mother had told her.

"So how are you, Natashia?" he asked.

"I am fine, just like I told you before," Natashia said with the directness of her ten years. And it was true – she already told him how she was outside the car and then on the way here.

"Yes, yes you did," Brad nodded, a little uncomfortable at Natashia's straightforward behavior.

Perhaps the hot weather was making him rethink the choice of his costume, Natashia wondered, as Brad fidgeted in his chair. She sat up straight as Brad asked her what she wanted to have for lunch.

"You pick," she said, just as her mom had taught her to say. Cece had drilled into her not to demand this or that thing and just go along with her father's choices. She wasn't allowed to make any demands on her father at all.

As the two of them waited for their order, Brad talked about his life in England and the weather there. Natashia wanted to ask him why he never took her mom there like he had promised, why he never married her, and why he had married another woman instead. She also wanted badly to ask why he never took care of her like he took care of his other kids.

However, she bit down on her tongue to stop those questions from slipping out. It was, once again, the strict instructions of her mother at work. Cece had told Natashia sternly to stick to polite and safe topics of conversations, adding that at the age of ten, Natashia was old enough to know what to talk about and what not to talk about with people.

"How are your children?" Natashia said after much thought. She couldn't find the right words for the question

first. She had thought to say 'my brothers and sister,' but then thought better of it – those four kids had not seemed like siblings to her at all.

"They are doing well," Brad said with a huge smile. He was obviously pleased that Natashia had asked about them.

As he launched into details of their school and hobbies and temperaments, Natashia wondered if he knew half as much about her, as he did about those other kids of his. Her thoughts wandered off to the ongoing bullying at school. She recalled how just this morning, one of those three mean sisters had cornered her in the school ground and asked if she had rubbed coal dust on her face this morning to look so ugly.

She opened her mouth to tell Brad about this, went so far as to say, *"You know what…"* But then, she gave up the idea. Her decision was made easy by Brad, who just ran over her words, continuing his story of how his daughter had ballet classes that he had to drive her to every weekend. He talked very fast and laughed easily, Natashia noticed. These two traits of her father stood out to her. Natashia nodded and smiled, politely at the right places. She even asked more questions about her half-siblings.

But she did not confront him about all the wrongs that he had done to her, his own daughter. The lunch ended, and he drove her back home. When Cece asked her how the outing went, Natashia shrugged and said it was all right. She didn't realize it yet, but she was learning the art of pretense way too early for her age.

***

It was a Sunday, and Natashia was, as usual, at her maternal grandmother's house. It was an island tradition to have huge family feasts on Sundays. The tradition was carried over from the days of slavery. Sunday was the Lord's Day when the slaves would rest and have a feast, after the week's hard work on the sugar plantations. It was a time for family and friends and abundant eating.

These meals were good preparation for the final Christmas feast that they had as a family. At the island, Christmas was a huge celebration. Usually, people would kill cattle or pigs, and then eat them over the holiday period. Natashia loved this time of the year, just as she loved the Sunday lunches because she always received gifts from her family. It was the only time other than her birthday that she got gifts so, of course, she loved it! The gifts were all piled around the Christmas tree, which was a hibiscus plant every year. They all had such fun decorating the tree two days before Christmas. It was a good use of the three-week vacation from school. She loved how the morning dew fell on the grass during Christmastime, how everything was white and dazzling. It was practically the only time of the year when the weather was cold on the island. Other than December, none of them ever wore sweaters. On Christmas Eve, they would all go to church, then after the mass, everyone would greet each other.

Then they would go house hopping on Christmas day. House hopping was a tradition at Christmas where they went to stay with their different relatives; it was just a way to share food and drink, as well as laughter and joys on Christmas. Last Christmas, Natashia had gotten a Barbie doll, something she had wanted for a long time. Nancy got a Barbie too, and Jack got a truck. Natashia's doll was blonde, slender, and white. She thought the doll looked like the white woman her mother used to work for when she was a child.

The children on the island usually played with white dolls. On the inside, however, the doll only reinforced her sense of inferiority. When alone, she would take out the doll and sit staring at her, quietly wishing she looked like the doll, so people would love her too. She even wanted to be transformed to look like Barbie, but she knew that would not happen. Natashia's grandmother used to take Jack, Nancy, and Natashia for grocery shopping every Saturday morning to get all the things to prepare for the big lunch. Natashia loved the bread and pastries, especially the ones called 'bun,' which was spongy, soft, and light colored. Nancy liked custard cakes, and Jack's favorite was hot bread with cheese.

Her grandmother preserved the freshness and hotness of the bread by wrapping it in cloth. By the time lunch was served, they all had a voracious appetite for all the delicacies. Their grandmother sometimes baked macaroni pie, cooked red kidney beans, chicken, beef, or mutton served with rice and a salad. They would have tropical fruit juices as drinks. For dessert, they had homemade mango ice-cream. This was the island custom – practically every household had such lunches on Sundays.

This Sunday, Natashia had started the day by playing games with Jack and Nancy, like she did each week. The time was getting close to lunch, and Natashia could almost hear her stomach rumbling. She took a break from playing and went inside the house to get a glass of water. As she walked inside the kitchen, she saw her mom talking to Aunt

Mary. The two of them were so engrossed in talking that they didn't notice Natashia enter. On her part, Natashia also kept as quiet as a cat because she didn't want them to enlist her for setting the table. She got her glass of water and downed it in big gulps. Then wiping her mouth with the back of her hand, she began to creep out the door. She quietly thanked her stars that she was out of the line of sight of her mother and aunt, who both had their backs to her.

Just as Natashia was about to exit the kitchen, she heard her mother speak her father's name. Natashia paused and then thought she should listen to whatever had happened. It never hurt to secretly learn all the things that adults kept from her was the way she thought.

The venom in Cece's voice had her knitting her brows. Whatever her dad had done now must have made her mom mad; but then, her dad always made her mom angry.

"But what did Brad say to you this time, Cece?" Mary asked the question Natashia had. *"He left the island a week ago, didn't he?"*

"Oh, he left," Cece said, chewing her words like bitter tobacco that she wanted to spit out. *"But before that, he*

showed, once again, what a bloody fool I was for falling into his trap!"

"Did he refuse to pay Natashia's expenses again?" Mary hazarded a guess.

"What's new with that? He has never taken financial responsibility for Natashia, has he?" Cece said.

"Well, then? Do you want me to keep guessing?" Mary said, starting to get annoyed with Cece's uncharacteristic tightlipped stance.

"It's so darn hard for me to even say it," Cece drew in a heavy breath then said it all at once, *"That bastard proposed that I rekindle...relations with him."*

"What?" Mary asked. She looked shocked.

"Exactly. I was as shocked as you are. But when I took some time to think it over, it wasn't shocking to me anymore. What else can you expect for a lowlife like Brad?"

"But still!" Mary sputtered. *"You are the mother of his daughter! The least he can do is show some respect for that."*

"As if he ever would," Cece snickered sarcastically. *"My one big regret in life is that he is the father of my daughter."*

Natashia watched both women from behind, not understanding, but at the same time understanding everything that was being said. She listened as her mom added, *"He came to the house so many times. Even when Natashia was at school. He told me he would contribute some money to help me with Natashia. I even took the money he offered the first few times. But then he started to suggest that maybe I should pay back...in other ways."*

"What the hell!" exclaimed Mary, banging the simmering pot of boiling rice with the dipper. Natashia jumped in her spot and then ducked to avoid being spotted. She thought she might as well listen to all the story.

Cece nodded bitterly. *"He thinks I would stoop so low and be one of those women that he takes to his rentals."*

Mary nodded her head enthusiastically in assent as if to second that, indeed, Brad was a pig. Stirring the contents of the pot, she added, *"The man has a wife and children in another country. And yet he strutted around like a peacock here, flashing those women, and dressed in those atrocious clothes to boot!"*

Cece nodded quietly, seemingly done with the conversation. She walked to get herself a glass of water, and

Natashia slipped out of the kitchen, feeling enraged on her mother's behalf. She was still seething at the insult that her father had delivered to her mother, as she went outside to rejoin Nancy and Jack. They were laughing and talking with each other, but Natashia didn't feel like joining in the fun anymore. She breathed a sigh of relief when she heard the loud voice of her grandmother, ordering them to come inside and wash up before sitting at the table.

Natashia took her seat and watched as her mother walked in with a steaming bowl of rice. The mouthwatering aroma of the fresh meal distracted Natashia from her new grief. She reached out to fill her plate with rice and chicken. She and Nancy exchanged a smile as they saw how Mary loaded up Jack's plate. When she was done, his plate had twice as much food as the two girls'. Jack had quite an appetite, and he loved eating. Natashia was secretly impressed by how much he could eat at one time.

The lunch continued with the mood of happiness, that was the norm on Sundays. Natashia laughed and joked with her cousins, forgetting the information she had learned about her father's behavior. She suppressed the knowledge of her dad's true character, so she wouldn't have to see how ugly the reality of the world was. It was her way of self-preservation; at her age, there was little else she could do to make life easier for herself. Her family didn't know, but she had too much on her plate already, with the incessant bullying at school, the truth of which came out for Cece, one day not too far in the future.

***

"Why are your grades falling, Natashia?" Cece asked her daughter after sitting her down one Friday evening.

Natashia bit down on her lip, noticing the very serious expressions on her mom's face. She could tell her mom meant business and wouldn't tolerate any deflections. She sat quietly as her mother watched her, willing her to answer the question.

"I have asked you a question, Natashia, haven't I?"

Natashia nodded. Cece added, *"Then tell me why a grade A+ student now brings in B's and C's, and even D's, in all the tests."*

"I don't know," Natashia said moodily. Even as she spoke the words, her mind was reeling with the happenings of the past year. Yes, her grades had dropped, and that was a result of deliberate efforts on her part.

From the perspective of a ten-year-old, Natashia had decided on the best strategy that she could come up with to sidestep bullying at school. She would no longer be the top student and so, would avoid the attention and hate of other kids. She had felt she was smart, so she was bullied more.

She had stopped focusing on her studies, knowing it wouldn't solve her problems. However, she had found out that more mediocre grades didn't stop the bullying. It only made her feel worse and made no impact whatsoever on the bullies, who now targeted her falling grades along with her complexion. The list of such nicknames as *"tar baby"* and *"Blackbird"* was extended to include *"dumb darkie"* and *"black-faced fool"*.

Tears gathered in Natashia's eyes as she recalled everything. Cece saw her daughter fighting back the tears. She sat down beside Natashia and asked her gently what was bothering her. Natashia could not resist her mother's soft words. She was coming to realize she wouldn't be able to handle the problem on her own. So she told everything to Cece – all the words those three sisters had said to her, the relentless misbehavior that she had to put up with, and the tormenting actions of the entire class that seemed to hate her.

Cece listened to her daughter patiently. Her face showed anger, but nowhere near as much as she felt. Cece's mind went back to the time when Natashia was first born. She was a tiny baby, dark, and with a tuft of hair in the middle of her head. She used to take Natashia to the health center for shots and checkups by bus. Every time she boarded the bus, there would be an old woman who would stare at Natashia and say rude things to Cece, such as, *"How did you bring such an ugly baby in the world?"*

Cece used to take the seat farthest from her and try her best to ignore the stares and comments that were loud enough to be overheard. She took that for two weeks before telling the woman off in a loud voice. After demonstrating her rage that one time, the woman never bothered her again. In a few months, she even stopped traveling by the same bus as Cece.

Two weeks was all it had taken for Cece to snap and here, her daughter had been taking bullying for so long. Cece decided to put her foot down and talk to the parents of the three bullies. The next day, she walked to their house and rapped on their front door. Declining their mother's invitation to come inside, she talked politely but firmly on the subject. She told the woman her three daughters had been bullying Natashia. The woman had called her daughters to Cece; their faces showed their guilt. Their mother had scolded them right in front of Cece and told her to stop bothering Natashia anymore. When Natashia returned from school the next day, her mother asked her about the bullying. She told her happily that the girls didn't bother her today, which was the first time in a very long time. In the days that followed, the three girls really didn't bother Natashia anymore.

However, the other kids whom the three sisters had recruited to bully her didn't stop. They persisted in their behavior, but Natashia ignored them, for the time being at least, because she was preoccupied with another matter entirely. She was experiencing the first crush of her life. There was a boy called Jem in her class. He was light-skinned and handsome. Moreover, he was friendly and polite to Natashia.

Not once had he ever bullied or even commented on her skin. He saw her as a friend and treated her like one. Every morning, he would exchange greetings with Natashia. Then he would ask her about school homework. The two of them often helped each other solve their math and English problems together. While Natashia was good at math, Jem was good at English. Together, they made a good team. So Natashia spent her days relaxed, happy to have made a close friend.

***

Natashia was eleven now. Soon, it was time for her to take the entrance exams for a high school. Cece wanted Natashia to attend the most prestigious of schools. But for that to happen, Natashia had to score really well in the exam. She had been working hard for it over the last few weeks. Cece was hopeful her daughter would make it to the top school, smart as she was.

Nancy and Jack were taking the exams too. When the results came out, Cece was ecstatic. Natashia made it to the best school on the island! Jack and Nancy attended a different school. Natashia was sad that she wouldn't study with her cousins, but she was also happy to have made her mother proud of her.

Around the same time, Brad visited the island again, once more without his wife and children. He took Natashia out on lunch, and there, Natashia asked him if his wife didn't like visiting the island. He did not agree with her, but Natashia noticed that he did not disagree either. Natashia wasn't surprised! Her father's wife looked very much like an outsider to Natashia, and it didn't look like she liked island life. It was no wonder she had not visited again after that first time. Natashia didn't mind that at all. If anything, she wanted to ask her dad to stop visiting as well. She wanted to tell him those visits did not make up for the lost time. However, she kept her silence, knowing all her words would fall on deaf ears.

Chapter 8 – New Beginnings

The next time Natashia saw her father was when he came down to the island at the time his grandmother died. This was Natashia's great-grandmother on the paternal side, and one of the first deaths that Natashia witnessed in her early life. For the first time, she confronted the reality of death – how it takes away people, so you can never ever see them again. Natashia wasn't quite close to the old lady, but she was still sad at her death.

After the funeral, Brad came to visit Natashia at her house. In his hands, there was a package which looked hastily wrapped in brown paper. Brad gave his signature broad smile, and handed Natashia the parcel, announcing, *"My wife thought you should have this. Go on, open it."*

Though Natashia didn't like the fact that it was Brad's wife, instead of him who had gotten her the present, she also felt a flutter of excitement like every child does on receiving a gift. She tried not to show her enthusiasm, however, and sat down on the sofa demurely. Then she began to open the gift wrap carefully, taking her time not to tear the creased plain brown paper. The wrapping finally fell away to reveal a... *"Is it a doll?"* Natashia asked, taken aback. She looked from her father to her mother, and both smiled at her in a rare moment of harmony. Brad nodded as Natashia sat still for a moment, not knowing what to do with the thing in her hand. It was a doll all right. Only it looked nothing like the dolls Natashia had seen in her lives. Dolls were supposed to be white. With a white and pink complexion and beautiful straight hair; but this doll was dark, just like her!

"It's a cabbage patch kid doll," Brad informed.

Natashia didn't understand what her father said, but she had already fallen in love with the doll. It had a chubby face and a dark brown complexion. Its hair was curly and looked wild – *"Just like mine!"* Natashia thought, barely stopping herself from jumping up and down with her newfound happiness.

"Here, look at this," Brad said, reaching inside the box. He extracted a small card from inside and handed it to Natashia, *"It's her birth certificate."*

Natashia looked at her father and asked, *"What's her name?"*

"You get to name it," Brad said.

"I do?" Natashia said, delighted. *"I will call her Nana."*

Cece, who had watched the entire proceedings from the side, commented, *"Say thank you to your father, Natashia."*

Natashia turned to her father and said, *"Thank you."* For the first time, she meant it. *"I love the doll. Please tell your wife I said thank you."*

Before Brad left, he handed over an envelope to Cece, who, as usual, took it reluctantly. *"It's to help with Natashia's school supplies,"* he said before waving them goodbye and driving away, pleased with all the big things that he, in his mind, had done for the two of them today.

After he left, Natashia retreated into her room with her new doll. She was in love with it. For the first time, she realized that dolls could look like her, too. While that fact didn't make her forget her dark complexion, it soothed some of the hurt that she always carried inside of herself like an always-throbbing bruise.

In the meanwhile, Cece counted the money Brad had given to her with his usual self-satisfied smirk. *"Two hundred dollars,"* she added up. This was nowhere near the amount she needed to fulfill Natashia's needs, but Brad apparently thought it would suffice. Resentment and bitterness rose insider her heart; he knew as well as she did how much it took to raise a child on the island and for him to give this much money to make for all the years that he had not financially supported his daughter's upbringing was only a joke. Cece let it go. She didn't expect anything from Brad, and nothing he did came as a surprise to her anymore.

***

Natashia quickly passed through the school corridor, ducking her head to avoid being seen from the principal's office. She clutched her book tightly to her chest and practically ran past the office and into the school ground, as it was the lunch hour.

"What's up with you?" Rita, her friend, asked.

"Nothing," Natashia mumbled. She didn't want to admit that she felt afraid of being called by the school principal. She had not even told her mother that the new principal at her school – an educated adult – called her "the black child". The first time he had done so, Natashia had felt more shocked than hurt. The feelings of humiliation had rolled over her like waves eventually. She looked up to the principal, like every kid in her class did. He was tall, slender, and had a light complexion.

He was also a very no-nonsense man. It was more like he spoke his mind without caring about other people's feelings, as Natashia had discovered. So she tried to avoid being in the principal's sight as much as she could. She didn't want him to call her 'the black child' and give sanction to the entire school to call her by the same name. Natashia sat under the shade of a palm tree and opened the book she had been carrying. It was a children's book called 'Oliver Twist.'

She loved reading about the little boy who had no mother, and who escaped from the workhouse and lived a tough but adventurous life. Following Oliver's story, chapter by chapter, made Natashia feel as if she weren't alone – as if there was another child like her who had a hard time finding true friends, and who battled with life's challenges every day.

Natashia, in truth, had found a refuge in the stories. Whenever she read, she could escape from the painful realities of her existence and pretend that her life, like that of her books' characters, will end on a happy note. Without her knowing it, she gained a sense of courage and determination from the books she read – the daring to persist in the face of all odds.

***

Summer arrived, and with it, Natashia found a much-needed break from school. This was her time to recover from the bullying that she endured practically every day. The best news was that after summer break would end, she would join a new school. This was the best high school on the island, and Natashia was quite happy that she would attend it. Right as her summer break began, she went with Cece to get a new uniform.

"Wow, it's so pretty!" Natashia exclaimed as the shopkeeper laid out the blue A-line skirt and a white top.

"It seems large for my daughter," Cece said to the shopkeeper, running her hand over the school logo stitched to the right breast of the blouse.

"Hmm...it is large. Or your daughter is small for her age," the man behind the counter commented. He asked Natashia to stand still while he took measurements to alter the uniform to her size. The skirt had to be shortened, and the shoulder width adjusted to fit her petite frame. Cece decided the date on which to collect the uniform from the shop and headed home after she picked up a new pair of black shoes and matching socks to go with Natashia's

uniform. This summer, before school started, seemed to be the longest of her life to Natashia. Though she felt a bit of anxiety in joining a new school, she was also very curious and looked forward to it. She had heard a lot of good things about the school. She hoped against hope to escape the misery of the regular bullying and make new friends who would love her for who she was, instead of targeting her skin color.

Natashia spent most of her days at the beach like she had done every summer of her life. The hours of the morning were taken up by running around and playing ball. Later, Natashia went for a swim, and after that, exhausted, she lay under the shade of the trees. A soft breeze was blowing, and sunlight glinted off the waves. There were not many people about at this time of the day.

Natashia watched the tranquil scene in front of her and closed her eyes. The warmth of the sun on her skin felt good, and she dozed off, tired as she was from swimming all day. A sharp stinging sensation on her arms jolted her awake from her nap. With her eyes still closed, she swatted her arm, thinking the mosquito would leave. That didn't happen, however. Natashia felt as if a hundred pins had stabbed her all at once.

In a matter of moments, she was wide-awake. She began to slap her arms furiously, but then she saw that it was not mosquitoes but bees. She let out a loud scream and got to her feet. The bees followed her as she rushed toward her cousins, hoping to outrun the insects, who seemed intent on piercing her skin. Someone had obviously left the hive loose, and the bees had swarmed around the spot where Natashia had unfortunately taken a nap.

Yelling for help, Natashia got closer to the beach where her cousins were still swimming. They watched her with puzzlement, not knowing why she was screaming like a banshee and running toward them with her arms wide open, as if she wanted to embrace them. Natashia entered the water, but that was the worst mistake she could have made.

As soon as the salty ocean water touched her skin, she felt agony worse than she had ever known before. Even when the glass bottle had broken and punctured her skin a few years ago, it had felt less painful than this. This was a sensation that can be compared to thousands of blades jabbing through the flesh. Jack and Nancy had swum up to her by that time. They carted a crying Natashia out of the water and lay her down on the sand.

"It's the bees. Look, the bees have stung her," Nancy commented, wincing as she saw the red welts that had begun to form on Natashia's skin.

"Look at her face," Jack said, grimacing at Natashia's bee-stung lips and cheeks.

It wasn't easy for Jack and Nancy to help Natashia back home. They half supported, half carried her. Cece let out a scream when she saw Natashia's face all swollen and red. Tears leaked from the corners of her daughter's eyes, who looked too drained to even cry. Cece put her down on clean sheets and proceeded to wipe off her skin with cold water. Natashia's grandmother arrived a few minutes later, alerted by Jack.

She checked up on her granddaughter and inspected the swelling with a deep frown on her face. Then she got to work. She asked for lemons and squeezed it all over Natashia's body, holding her down as she fought to avoid the citric acid of the fruit. Natashia's skin burned as if a fire was lit underneath it. She wanted to scratch the itches, but her mother held her hands, telling her that if she scratched, it would itch more. The tickling sensation from the lime subsided after thirty minutes, and the bee sting also lessened in intensity but did not entirely vanish. All night, Natashia tossed and turned, unable to go to sleep properly, though her eyelids felt heavy as boulders. The next day, Natashia stayed home to recover. The stinging pain disappeared in two days but left bruises on her body. Natashia prayed that the scars would fade away before school began. She had her dark skin to worry about already; she didn't want the ugly scars on her body, as she knew it would give people more reason to bully her.

***

Summer was not over yet. Natashia's cousin Lily, who was the daughter of one of her aunts who lived in the city, visited her grandmother's place. Natashia got along well with Lily, and so did Jack and Nancy. Lily was a good sport and was always joking around.

One afternoon, they were playing outside, like they did every day. Lily ran toward Natashia with the old wheelbarrow. Usually, all the kids loved riding in the wheelbarrow but always behind their grandmother's back. It was because grandma had told them the cart was old and rusty, and it wasn't safe to ride it. They loved it, though, and they took turns pushing each other around in it.

The wheelbarrow had no passenger at present. Lily was pushing the empty cart around, and she thought it would be a good idea to scare Natashia. Laughing as if it were the biggest joke, Lily ran toward Natashia; she obviously wanted to scare her cousin by making her think she would run her over with the wheelbarrow. Natashia saw Lily rushing toward her with the wheelbarrow, and she stepped out of her path neatly; she was practiced at this game already.

Lily grinned and asked, *"Who wants to ride it now?"*

They took turns pushing each other, and this time, Jack raised his hand. He got into the small cart, long limbs and all, and Lily began to push him around. Laughing, she moved fast to give Jack an enjoyable jaunt. Jack was laughing, too. But then, suddenly Lily stopped pushing and fell down on the ground. She clutched her left side, as her cousins gathered around her.

"Ouch, Lily! You dropped me!" Jack said, climbing out of the fallen cart and examining his elbows for any scratches that he may have received. Nancy and Natashia laughed at Jack and peered at Lily, to see if she up on her feet and laughing at Jack as she liked to do every time she got the

better of him. But Lily was still on the ground, crying out in pain.

"Come on! Stop joking, Lily!" Jack said as he nudged her with his foot.

Nancy and Natashia approached her, beginning to fear that something really had happened to their cousin, and that it wasn't one of her practical jokes.

"What happened, Lily? What happened?" Natashia asked, sitting down on the ground beside Lily. Lily's state almost sent Natashia into a state of panic. It looked to her that Lily would die. She was bent double in pain and gasping for breath. Tears were streaming out of her eyes that she had closed in pain.

Nancy put her hand on Lily's arm and asked again, *"Open your eyes, Lily. Tell us what's wrong?"* At the back of her mind was also the fear of her grandmother, who she knew would come outside at any moment.

Natashia stood to the side, feeling helpless, and not knowing what to do. Just yesterday, Lily had pretended to be injured and had laughed at them when they'd fallen for her trick. This time, though, Natashia knew that something was terribly wrong with Lily for real.

Although Lily loved to cry wolf, this time the wolf really was here. When the pain didn't stop, Lily began to scream louder. Her face was covered in tears. Jack, Nancy, and Natashia watched her, afraid of what would happen to Lily but also worried about what would happen to them. They knew they were not allowed to push each other in the wheelbarrow.

In only a matter of minutes, Grandmother came out of the house, running. *"What happened here?"* she asked, bewildered. She grabbed Lily and turned her small body to look at what was wrong.

Natashia, Jack, and Nancy looked at each other, guiltily. Then Jack said, *"We....we were playing with the wheelbarrow. Lily was pushing me around, and then she suddenly fell."*

Nancy added, *"We don't know what happened, grandma. She was just fine, but then she started crying."*

Their grandmother looked at her with anger in her eyes. She didn't scold them, however, and ordered them to help her carry Lily inside the house. After Lily was put in bed, moaning in pain, their grandmother wagged her finger at them, *"I will see to you three later. Sit down and pray for Lily to be all right, or there will be hell to pay for you three."*

After telling them off, she went out into her garden. A while later, she marched back inside with a few leaves clutched in her hand.

"Bush medicine," Natashia said, nudging Nancy with her elbow. Nancy nodded. They both knew their grandmother was an expert on bush medicine, but somehow, whatever the matter was with Lily didn't seem like it could be cured by the homemade brew.

Grandma went into the kitchen and began boiling the leaves. After some time, she added a pinch of salt in it. When the concoction was made, she poured it into a glass and took it to Lily. Natashia watched from the room's doorway, as Grandma tried to coax a weeping, protesting Lily to drink the medicine.

Lily gagged at the smell of the green brew in the glass. She mustered all her strength and resisted being force-fed the nauseating mixture. She jerked her head from side to side, and the medicine went more on her clothes and face than into her mouth. The medicine was half down Lily's throat when she began vomiting. Grandmother rubbed her back, now thoroughly worried, as the three of them watched anxiously from the side.

"We have to take her to the hospital," Grandmother announced finally.

Aunt Mary and Cece arrived after a while, and all of them took Lily to the hospital. Grandmother was apprehensive about sending the news to her daughter in the city, whose child Lily was.

"She sent Lily here with trust that we would take care of her. Now, look what you've done!" Cece yelled at all three of them. She promised to give them the beating of their life when they got home.

"Sorry," Jack said, hanging his head. In truth, none of them had expected this to happen. They had been using that cart for quite a long time now, and nothing had ever gone wrong. They knew their cousin Lily was in terrible pain, and they felt remorseful for what she was going through.

"We will have to operate on her immediately," the doctor informed them after inspecting Lily. *"She is in a critical condition. How did the accident happen?"*

Jack hesitated before he revealed, *"She was pushing me around in our old wheelbarrow. Then I guess the* wheelbarrow hit a stone in the ground or something because I felt the bump. Then Lily fell to the ground."

The doctor nodded and said, "I see. It makes sense. It must be the handle of the wheelbarrow then. The impact of it on her skin pierced her small intestine. You did the right thing bringing her in now. If you had waited till morning, she probably wouldn't have survived."

As the operation was done, Natashia and the others waited, fearful of what might happen. In a couple of hours, Lily was operated on successfully and shifted to the general ward. She was out of danger and also out of pain. Natashia went in to see her with Jack and Nancy. She was asleep by then. The rest of the summer, poor Lily was confined to the hospital where she had to stay to recuperate. They visited her often, still feeling guilty for what they had inadvertently put her through.

***

Summer was at a close. The time to join the new school was approaching. Just before the session started, Natashia asked Nancy to tell her what to expect from the high school which, frankly, intimidated her the nearer she got to joining it.

Nancy went to a different school, but Natashia believed she must have an idea about how things went on at high school that were different from primary schools. She bombarded Nancy with questions about the classes, the teachers, and the class fellows.

"And what about the principal? Do you think the principal will be nice there? How is the principal at your school?" Natashia asked anxiously. In her mind came the image of her primary school principal, standing at his full height and calling her by the degrading title of *"the black child"*. It wasn't so much the words, but the tone in which he said it that had wounded Natashia; she had not recovered from the insult still and doubted that she ever would.

"Relax, Natashia! Everybody is going to be great at your school, I am sure. There are a few bad apples, but you have those everywhere, even at my school. I am sure you will make great friends soon," Nancy reassured her in the manner of a big sister, which she really was to Natashia.

"Well, at least I won't have to see the faces of the mean sisters," Natashia said. This was one of the biggest boons of switching schools for Natashia: she would no longer have to see the faces of her torturers every working day of the week.

"Yes!" Nancy said, high-fiving her cousin. The truth was that she was glad for Natashia. Not only was she moving to a much better school but was getting a clean slate as well. The new school, Nancy hoped in her heart, would give Natashia a fresh start, and if all went well, the people there wouldn't judge her for her skin color and see the beautiful and smart person her cousin was.

Natashia, too, hoped the new school would give her a new beginning – where she could be who she was without being ashamed of and mocked for being a dark-skinned girl in a white, white world.

Chapter 9 – Taking a Stance

Natashia clasped her shaking hands together and took a deep breath. Then she entered through the gates of her new school – St. Mary's School. Looking straight ahead, she kept walking. She held her head high, and her nose was in the air; she had her shoulder pushed back, giving people the impression that she was, perhaps, arrogant or prepared to pick a fight with whoever dared to cross her.

From her appearance, no one could tell that her heart was trembling with the fear of rejection. The bullying she had endured so far in her life made her feel unwelcome wherever she went.

And so it did at this school.

"I endured the three sister bullies before; I can get through this, too. I can get through this!" Natashia said to herself over and over again. She thought if she said it enough times, she would believe the words.

She passed other students, and their faces did not register in her mind – only their grins and carefree laughter.

"They don't expect to be rejected like me," Natashia mused. And it was true – the lifelong bullying over her skin color had instilled a sense of inferiority in her. She thought others would be accepted, and she wouldn't be – and with good reason. She stood to the side of the hall, her back to the wall, waiting for the assembly announcement. That's when she'd find out who her classmates would be, as well as her teachers.

In a few minutes, a stick-thin woman approached the front of the hall with a folder clutched against her chest. Pushing her glasses up her nose, she loudly announced, *"Now, all students should get here in line. Yes, stand like good little soldiers."* With the announcement, all the students rushed into the hall and began to form lines. Natashia felt disoriented for a moment, and then she followed the horde.

Someone from the staff told her the row for her class, and she joined it, standing behind a girl who was almost a half-foot taller than her. Since this was the first assembly, no one took care to line up according to their heights. From the back, Natashia saw that the girl in front of her had thick black hair and a brown complexion – not white but shades lighter than her.

As the teachers waited for all the students to gather into their respective rows, Natashia shifted from one foot to the other. She was impatient for some reason; besides, the girl in front of her was blocking her view, and she had to look around her to see the dais. As she craned her neck, she heard two girls who were standing in the row beside hers whisper furiously. From the corner of her eyes, she saw one of them point to her. Natashia stood straight. She didn't look at them but could tell they were laughing at her. *"Is it my shoes? My bag? My color?"* Natashia wondered. It could be any of those things – or all of them.

Natashia had spotted at first sight that the students who came to this school were rich – well, richer than her at least. It showed in the confident smiles they wore, their shiny shoes, and their expensive schoolbags. As the finger-pointing and whispering continued, Natashia began to lose the poise she had taken such pains to assume this morning. All her nervousness returned. The orientation and the day had barely started, but she could not wait for it to be over. A few minutes later, the staff of the school began to approach the dais. Natashia barely heard the teachers' and the principal's introductions, she was so distracted.

All around her, she listened to the students clap and laugh – they were all so enthusiastic and cheerful. Not her, though! *"They are so noisy,"* Natashia thought as she tried to regain her composure. Ignoring the speech that the principal was delivering, Natashia pulled her bag in front of her and stared at it. It looked okay to her, but it had no pictures like on the bags of other students. Her uniform, she knew, was crisp and clean. Her mother had gotten her black socks to go with her black shoes – this was the complete dress code of the school which had to be followed, or else they would send you home.

"You have to live up to the school's standards," Cece had told her last night, instructing her to be on her best behavior. She had also told her to make friends quickly – *"That's the best way, Natashia,"* she had said, *"Make friends on the first day because it only gets tougher as time passes."*

"And who can I make friends with her?" she wondered, listening to the other girls whisper not only about her but about others too. They commented on the other students' faces, their appearance, and anything else that could be a marker of social class. Looking at the students of a prestigious school behave in this discriminating manner had disheartened Natashia. She felt no desire to strike up a conversation with any of them, let alone to make friends with

them. Natashia was still immersed in the thoughts of how she would survive in this place without friends when the opening ceremony was concluded. She quickly clapped her hands along with the other students. Then the time came for them to enter their classrooms.

Natashia was walking in the line to the class when the girl who had stood in front of her turned around. Giving a big smile, she said to Natashia, *"Hi! I am Nathalie. And you?"*

Natashia was taken aback. She had not expected the tall girl to greet her. So it took a few moments for her to form a response. Nathalie waved her hand in front of Natashia, and she quickly said, *"Hello, I am Natashia!"*

"Nice to meet you! You seem so tiny to me, are you sure you are in this class?" Nathalie said.

Natashia was so sensitive to people's words by now that she thought Nathalie was making fun of her small stature. But when she looked at her classmate, she saw that she wasn't mean. Natashia's natural spiritedness came out. She said, *"You are too tall for this class!"*

Nathalie put her hand on her mouth and giggled, *"I know! My mum told me to stop growing last year, but I didn't listen to her."*

At that moment, Natashia knew she would be friends with Nathalie. She could laugh at herself, and she was kind. An additional feature was that she wasn't light-skinned. Natashia had nothing against fair skinned girls, but most of such people she had come across so far at school had bullied her to no end. They acted so superior because of their complexion, which wasn't something they could take credit for in the first place.

Natashia stepped into the classroom behind Nathalie and followed her to the seat. Taking her place beside her new friend, she looked around. Nathalie seemed to be an outgoing, social girl – Natashia knew that because she was busy making friends with the other classmates. When everyone was seated, Natashia silently counted: there were around thirty students in the class, and most of them looked well-off from their appearance.

Before the teacher entered the class, Natashia also made a quick mental note of the fair skinned girls in the class. They all seemed to be sitting together, indicating they had formed a group of their own. For a minute, Natashia felt a desire to join their group and be their friend. They all looked so pretty to her, and so lucky. However, as one of those fair, pretty girls glanced at Natashia and murmured in her friend's ears,

Natashia gave that idea up. She would not even dream of being friends with people who talked about her in a derogatory manner, and who made fun of her skin. In a sense, Natashia accepted that though her school had changed, in some ways, the old bullying would continue. By the end of the day, it became more apparent to Natashia where she stood. The students and most of the teachers were biased against her. She knew it because very few of her classmates talked to her, and all but one of her teachers refused to call on her in the class.

She saw that even her teachers smiled at the lighter-skinned girls; when they looked at Natashia, their smiles seemed forced. Natashia also saw the teachers look at her with a frown of puzzlement, as if they could not comprehend how this dark little girl, who looked to be from the wrong side of the tracks, had made it to this prestigious school. Olive, Tanya, and Veronica were three other friends that Natashia made by the end of her first day at school.

These girls were all various shades darker than the lighter-skinned girls. None of them were anywhere close to a lighter complexion. Plus, they were so funny and friendly that they made Natashia feel right at home. She felt excited already to tell her mother about the new friends she had made on the first day of school.

***

A few weeks had passed since Natashia had joined her new school. She had adjusted to the routine, though sometimes the thoughtless, cruel remarks of her schoolfellows got to her. The bullying still happened, but with her group of friends around to support her, Natashia had found a way to cope with it. Her self-esteem took hits, but she never let it show. She knew how to put a brave front, how to look strong and to never cry in front of those who thought her as weak and inferior.

It was around this time that Brad visited the island again. Like the last time, he had come alone. And like always, he had told Cece he would pick Natashia up from her school and take her out – *"For an ice-cream?"* Natashia had looked at her mom. *"What else?"* Cece had shrugged.

Natashia rolled her eyes. You could call her dad predictable, or someone who liked sticking to routines. However, Natashia saw it as not putting in any effort and getting away with doing the bare minimum. That is how Brad had always treated Natashia.

The next day when school was over, Natashia walked out the main doors and saw her dad waiting by a white rental car. She politely said hello to him and hopped inside, making well-mannered inquiries about his family back home.

Brad said, *"You have changed schools, I see. Your mother told me the address of this one when I called her."*

Natashia only nodded and gave no explanation about how she had made it to one of the most notable schools on the island, and how that was a significant achievement for someone like her who had not had a privileged upbringing. Her dad had never expressed an interest in Natashia's life and her accomplishments, and she wasn't about to tell him when he had no curiosity whatsoever about his own daughter.

"Let's get you an ice-cream!" Brad announced with a grin as if he were talking to a child. He seemed to have forgotten Natashia's age, or maybe he thought that getting her an ice cream was the highest favor he could confer on Natashia.

Natashia sat down at the same table they always took.

"So you are in high school now?" he asked.

"Yes."

"You don't seem to be a very talkative girl. My daughter, though…you remember her? She talks a lot! She chews my ears off, talking all the time," Brad laughed. He said it in such a way that made it clear to Natashia that he thought he had only one daughter – the one he had left back home. Natashia was nowhere in the list of his kids. Though she was hurt by his words, she said nothing. Like her mother, she had taught herself to expect the least from her father. As it was, he even failed those low expectations when the time came for it.

Brad launched into a tale of his job in England, and Natashia nodded. The hour ended, and he drove Natashia to her home. She breathed a sigh of relief. These meetings were nothing but a pain for her. She came out of a sense of duty, and because somewhere in her mind, was the notion that she should have some sort of relationship with her father.

When Brad dropped her off, he got out of the car to greet Cece.

Natashia excused herself and went inside the house to change. Cece, in the meanwhile, remained at the door. Out of manners, she invited him inside, though she really didn't want to entertain him. She was relieved when he declined the offer.

Clearing her throat, Cece said, *"You know Natashia is in high school?"*

"Yeah, she just told me," Brad answered.

Saying the next words cost a lot to Cece, but she still did. *"So... the school is very prestigious. The cost of books and school supplies, and the fee...it is all very high."*

Brad's face showed indifference. He shrugged and said, *"Yeah, I guess so. Maybe you should get her to change schools. It isn't easy to pay for a good school. I know it because of my kids in England."*

Cece did not say a word after that. It was already quite tough for her to ask Brad for help. But, like her sister Mary had told her, it was Brad's duty to contribute to his daughter's expenses. So she had asked him for help. And now she felt humiliated at his disinterest and having asked him of all people. She should not have said a word to him and held onto her dignity. Swallowing her pride to talk to him about her expenses had got her nowhere. Watching Brad drive off in his car, Cece thought to herself, *"Got nothing but what I asked for!"*

***

One afternoon, Natashia came home and saw that her Aunt Mary was with her mother. This was rather odd because her aunt did not usually visit at this time of the day. Cece told Natashia to change and have her lunch while she talked to her sister of important matters. Naturally, Natashia perked up her ears. She stood outside her mother's room to eavesdrop on the conversation between her aunt and her mother. She could hear every word, but it took her some time to make sense of the plot.

"Tommy stirred up all this trouble! What else can we expect of him?" Cece accused.

Now, Natashia knew her mother had never been on good terms with her brother Tommy. She never quite understood why; Uncle Tommy was fine with her. He laughed and talked to her like he did with all his nephews and nieces. He didn't speak to Cece, though. Natashia thought he was so handsome with his light skin and tall height. Of course, she had heard stories from her mother's early life when Cece had had serious fights with Uncle Tommy.

Cece said Tommy used to argue over everything with her and wanted the best of everything, leaving nothing for his sisters.

"Just because he's the only son, he thinks he should have everything," Mary shook her head.

"He'll find out it's not so easy," Cece promised.

Mary shrugged and added, *"That land belongs to all of us. He can't just come and lay claim to everything."*

"And he dared to tell us not to visit grandmother!" Cece said. She was referring to the time that Tommy had ordered the entire family to leave Natashia's great-grandmother alone.

"We should have understood then what was on his mind," Mary remarked.

"Now he has got the land dispute going again. He wants all the money, so he could have his lavish lifestyle – his cars and his women," Cece said sarcastically.

Mary sighed and said, *"I just don't want the police involved this time like before."*

"But he had threatened grandmother to give the papers of the land to him! What is he going to stop at, Mary?" Cece exclaimed.

Natashia's brows furrowed. She recalled hearing some of this history a few years ago. The story was that after the emancipation on the island, the family had got about 800 acres of land. They didn't particularly care about dividing up the land between the heirs and lived peacefully on the island. It was all in the family, after all. But now it seemed that Uncle Tommy wanted all the land for himself, without giving anybody else their lawful share.

"I am going to see how he takes it away from us," Cece said. Also, when she said anything in that tone, Natashia knew that her mother would have her way.

In the next few days, Natashia saw how Cece did precisely as she had said. She enlisted the extended family for help, and with them on their side, she was able to thwart Tommy's efforts to grab the land for himself. Natashia was kind of proud of her mother for standing up for what was right and what was hers. Natashia absorbed this lesson and would demonstrate the same grit as her mother had in the times to come.

Chapter 10 – England

"Mr. Diaz, I know the answer!" Natashia exclaimed, raising her hand, almost leaping from her seat in her excitement to be chosen.

Mr. Diaz, the math teacher at the high school, smiled and pointed at Natashia who triumphantly rose from her chair. *"X is equal to five!"*

"Correct!" Mr. Diaz grinned and gestured Natashia to sit back on her seat, which she did with no small hint of pride. The class continued. Natashia participated actively in math class and tried to solve the problems before anybody else. It was not only because she loved math as a subject, but because Mr. Diaz, who was from South America, was her favorite teacher.

He was one of the only few teachers at the school, who did not discriminate against Natashia because she was dark-skinned. Contrary to her expectations, teachers at this prestigious school, too, had their prejudices. Natashia was still trying to become accustomed to it. When the class ended, Natashia collected her books and put them in her bag. It was lunchtime. She walked out of the class with Nathalie and her other friends following. In the hall, she saw Kathy, and a bright smile lit her face.

"Hey Kathy!" she called out, running to her friend.

Kathy turned around, and Natashia was once more struck by her beauty. Kathy was light-skinned and had long brown hair. Her mother had married Cece's distant cousin, and so the two of them were related. *"Hi, Natashia. Wanna come to eat lunch?"* she asked.

Natashia invited Kathy to sit with her and Nathalie at lunch. Kathy was in the same grade but a different homeroom group, so all of them were friends but could only hang out together during lunchtime. Looking at Kathy out of the corner of her eyes, Natashia briefly considered telling her of her cousin, Jack's interest in her. Jack had asked countless questions about Kathy – whether she had a boyfriend and would she consider going out with him if she didn't.

Natashia dropped the idea because she knew her friend, Kathy, was studious and wanted nothing to do with boys. As she ate her lunch and joked with her friends, Natashia's thoughts inevitably went to the other girls of the school, and she frowned, thinking about their rumored illicit relationships with bus drivers and men. They would gather in the girl's toilet and tell tales of who had kissed whom and when. It was true that those girls went behind their parents' back and flirted with much older males. One of them had even become pregnant and had to drop out of school a few months ago. Natashia did not belong to that group of girls, who were ready to throw away their future for temporary, meaningless flings. Natashia knew how vital it was to have an education; her mom had drilled it into her head from childhood.

Besides, she knew how Cece had never got the chance to complete her education because of poverty, hardship, and family responsibilities; so she wanted to fulfill Cece's dream by becoming highly educated herself. She never much mingled with the group of wild girls, as her mom referred to them. It wasn't that she hated them, or she feared they would influence her to do what they did; in all truth, she was only scared about her mom finding out.

She knew there would be hell to pay if Cece ever discovered Natashia associated with girls who threw caution to the wind and did as they pleased while betraying their parents' trust. Pushing up her thick glasses up her nose, Natashia chattered unstoppably with Kathy. The two of them got along excellently. Natashia loved the fact that Kathy never teased her or had ever called her any name, even as a joke. Kathy loved how plucky Natashia was, and in a way, looked up to her for taking a stand for herself. Just a month ago, Natashia had got her glasses. A new round of vicious bullying had begun; this time, the bullies targeted Natashia's glasses. Kathy had seen how her friend had refused to budge, though she hated being called names for her poor eyesight. She ignored the bullies and wore her eyeglasses proudly, even defiantly. And now nobody bothered her because she simply didn't seem to care.

"Listen!" Natashia whispered as she leaned close to Kathy and nudged her.

"What?" Kathy whispered back.

"Do you know what a trainer bra is?"

"Of course," Kathy said, smiling. *"I wear one."*

"Oh, I thought you would. Since you're bigger than me and all," Natashia said, considering. *"It's just, I think I should wear one, too."*

"Yeah, so why don't you ask your mom?" Kathy suggested.

"I will," Natashia said.

After she went home that day, she told Cece what she wanted. She was surprised when Cece pulled out a trainer bra from the cupboard. *"I got this for you a while ago,"* Cece said. *"I was just waiting for when you might want to try it on."*

The next morning, Natashia wore the bra to school, but it was a nightmare. The bullies spotted her, and they spent chanting for the rest of the day, *"Blackbird is wearing a bra!"* Natashia felt humiliated. She didn't know what to do to make them stop. She came to school the next day without the bra, but in a week, she realized that if it weren't one thing, the bullies would find another thing to tease her about. She gave up trying to get them off her back, as she realized the more she tried, the harder they would bully her.

***

It was a few months after Natashia's fourteenth birthday that Brad revisited the island. After the customary trip to the ice cream parlor, which thoroughly bored Natashia, he dropped her home. Natashia was running inside the house after saying a quick goodbye to her dad when he called to her to stay put. He turned to Cece and said to her, *"I won't* be able to spend weeks at the island next summers." Cece suppressed the urge to shrug and said, "Sure. Suit yourself."

"Why?" Natashia peered from behind her mother, who was standing in the doorway and asked. She was fine with the idea of her dad not visiting, but she was still curious why he was breaking the tradition he had established.

"I have work," he answered shortly.

Unlike Cece, Natashia did shrug nonchalantly, telling her dad she didn't care if he came or not, without any words spoken. As Cece quelled her laughter, Brad rolled his eyes and said, "So I have a different idea. How about you come to visit me?"

"What?" Natashia said.

"Yeah, visit me in England. I will get the paperwork done. You will get a new experience."

"Oh," Natashia said. She couldn't say much because she was baffled. It wasn't like her dad to be so generous with her.

Brad told them that he would pick Natashia up on the weekend to get her picture taken so that her passport could be made. He left after discussing the plan some more with

Cece. As soon as he was gone, Natashia said, *"I don't think he's really going to take me, mum."*

"Yeah, me neither," Cece said bluntly. In her experience, Brad never followed through on what he said. *"Wait till next year."*

***

When summers came, Brad made good on his promise, to Cece's utter surprise. She helped Natashia pack her bags for England, silently marveling at the change, if it really was one, in Brad.

Natashia stood inspecting the contents of the bag, making sure her cabbage patch doll was in there. Though she knew she was too old for the doll, she loved it so much that she couldn't bear to part from it for the entire summer.

"When will I be back?" she asked her mom.

"By summer's end before your school begins. I told Brad to ship you to the island a week before classes start, at least," Cece answered, folding a newly-bought jacket, and putting it at the top of the pile before zipping the bag closed.

"I will miss you, mom," Natashia said.

"I'll miss you, too," Cece said briskly and left the room. She didn't want to become emotional over her daughter leaving. In all her fifteen years, Natashia had never lived away from her, save for her annual visits to her grandmother's house. And now that she was leaving for a far-off country, Cece felt clueless. Her life had revolved around her daughter for so long that she didn't know how she'd spend her time with Natashia gone for two months.

Shaking away her miserable thoughts, she called out, *"Go to sleep now, Natashia!"*

"Why?" came the impudent answer. Cece rolled her eyes; she wasn't surprised. Natashia hardly ever obeyed her without asking questions and satisfying her own logical sense.

"Because your flight is at 9 in the morning! Your dad will be here at 6. I'll wake you up at 5. Is that a good enough reason?" Cece shouted back, so Natashia would hear it in the room.

"Yeah, I guess so!" Natashia answered cheekily.

After a while, the lights inside the room were turned off, and Natashia closed the door halfway. Cece watched from the lounge as her daughter got into bed. Giving Natashia sufficient time to fall asleep, she walked into the bedroom and stood beside the bed that she shared with the daughter. In the faint moonlight that fell on Natashia's face through the open window, Cece saw the peace on her face. She was still a child and slept like one. Cece pushed Natashia's hair away from her face and tucked the blanket snugly around her.

***

The next morning, Natashia flew to England with her dad accompanying her. Brad had come down to the island to take Natashia with him, as this was her first time ever of traveling out of her birthplace. The flight was ten-hour long. After making some attempts at conversation, Brad leaned back in his chair and fell asleep.

Ignoring his snoring, Natashia glanced around the plane. She saw that there were all sorts of people traveling with her: black and white and all the shades in between. She wondered if the people in England – who, from her knowledge, were all white like the snow – would think she was too ugly to be in their country. Would they make fun of her? Would they point their fingers at her skin color? Would they laugh at her if she walked down the streets? She shuddered, thinking of all the horrible possibilities. She had read about England in books. She knew it was one of the islands that were part of the United Kingdom. The people who Cece worked for were British, and they were kind and friendly, so that gave Natashia some hope that it might not be so bad. She peeked at her dad's face. He was asleep, with his mouth hanging slightly open. Though he looked quite ridiculous at the moment, Natashia knew he fit the standard of beauty on the island.

He wasn't dark like her but was a golden-brown color; it made him look deeply tanned, and it was the reason why so many women were still attracted to him. Her mom was also brown-skinned. It was her paternal great-grandmother, she had learned, who was as dark as midnight, just as Natashia was. 'What misfortune!' Natashia often used to wonder, 'That I took after the one great grandma.'

***

The plane landed at Heathrow Airport. After the usual routine, Natashia walked out into a world that appeared brand-new and shining to her novice eyes. Brad's wife and daughter had come to pick them up. Natashia greeted them quietly and smiled, though she could see the wife was not too excited to see her. She hugged Natashia and said,

"Welcome to London. How was your flight?"

"It was good," Natashia said with a smile.

She walked out of the airport, tagging after her father and stepmother. Her sister walked quietly beside her. After the sandy beaches, palm trees, tropical climate, and wide open skies of the island, London looked like a different universe altogether. The temperature was much milder, and the sun looked pale and weak.

Natashia was wearing jeans and a t-shirt, the clothes they usually wore here in England. Though it was summer here, the weather seemed chilly to Natashia by comparison. She wished that she had carried her jacket instead of putting it in her bag.

"We'll get home in time for lunch," Brad said, lugging the small suitcase.

Natashia nodded in answer. She was too busy observing and absorbing her new surroundings to talk. She got in the cab, and the first thing she noticed on the drive homeward was the squeaky clean road. Really, it was nothing like what she saw on the island! The buildings here were tall, the streets all tidy, and the pedestrians all walked with a sense of purpose.

It took an hour to reach the house. The way looked something right out of a movie to Natashia. There were double bridges, four lanes, and skyscrapers that seemed to touch the clouds. She also saw the police guards standing at ease in different places, dressed in their famous red and black dresses. She wanted to wave to them in excitement but stopped in time; she did not want her father's family to think she was weird! She wondered if this trip was Brad's way of making up for all the things he had never done for his daughter. She gave up thinking about it after a while, though, as she knew she would not find an answer to this question.

That night, she didn't sleep. She was missing her mother, Jack, Nancy, and practically all her family! When the morning came, she hopped out of bed. Her stepmother made her an English breakfast –pancakes with syrup on it along with a tall glass of orange juice. Now, this Natashia liked! It was very different from the food she ate at home.

After breakfast was over, Brad's wife Olive told Natashia to get ready for the mall. Natashia was a little intimidated by the thought of heading out with a woman she barely knew, but she complied. She was very curious to see the shopping mall here. Besides, she could hardly say no to her host.

"Oh, my God! This looks huge!" Natashia exclaimed as soon as they reached the mall. And it was huge! Natashia had not been inside a building this sprawling before.

Her half-sister Uma laughed, though it was not a mean laugh. Natashia joined in her laughter.

Olive smiled and said, *"This is the biggest shopping mall in London."*

"It's pretty cool," Uma added seriously.

"It looks very cool!" Natashia said eagerly. She couldn't wait to explore the place.

She thoroughly enjoyed her time at the mall. At the end of the day, she'd seen hundreds of things she had never seen before. The clothes, the gadgets, the accessories – everything was so modern and different than at home! Natashia tried on different dresses but bought only one. She looked at so many expensive things but did not dare to desire them because she knew she could not afford it.

Her four hours at the mall were made better by the fact that all the strangers at the mall appeared super-friendly to her. Every time their eyes met with Natashia's, they smiled and nodded at her. Maybe they guessed she was a tourist. She ate a dinner of fast food – burger and fries with a coke. She saved all the memories because she wanted to tell Jack and Nancy precisely what everything was like here in London.

"There are mostly white people here, but many people of different ethnicities also live in the city," Olive informed her.

Natashia nodded. She could see as much for herself at the shopping mall.

In the days that followed, Natashia learned to have a good time in London. She would go out to cycle with her half-sister and go to the mall or the movies. Uma introduced her to rap music, and the two of them would get out of breath, singing along with the songs over and over again. This glimpse into a novel world was breathtaking for Natashia for the first few days.

Early morning a few days later, Natashia saw the changing of the Guard at Buckingham Palace. She was surprised and exhilarated to see it was a proper ceremony. Starting with the beat of the drum, she tried to memorize all the details, so she could share it with Jack and Nancy later.

She liked one particular group the most, and when her father asked her why, she said, "Because of their red shirts and their funny caps!" Brad laughed and told her they were called the Foot Guard. She realized that here in this country, she could learn so much of history just by visiting different places. Later, she saw the Tower of London, which was, by far, the most regal building she had ever seen in her life!

"Maybe a king lived here..." she wondered out loud. Uma told her that this tower by the River Thames was actually a fortress built for protection a thousand years ago. Her mouth hung slightly open as she listened to the chronicle of the place. The moat fascinated her to no end, and she could not believe her eyes when she saw the opulent rooms inside. Who knew wealth like this had ever existed in the world!

Natashia also went to the famous Hyde Park one Saturday evening. Her father's wife had packed a picnic. Playing on the rolling grounds of the park with her half-sister, she had the time of her life. This place was nothing like the warm, sandy beaches of the island, but she loved it here all the same.

When Natashia experienced the snow falling in summer, she was mesmerized. Growing up in her tropical hometown, she had never even seen snow before. She felt the peculiar sensation of snowflakes melting in her hand. She loved all of it and knew there would be no other feeling like this first sight of falling snow. In time, she got well-adjusted to life here, which she saw was much easier, convenient, and faster than life back home. Though his father tried to be very friendly, and his wife was civil and hospitable, Natashia knew they were very much like the people of the island in what they thought of her dark skin.

They never said it to her face, but Natashia knew from the things she overheard – their remarks when watching the television, their jokes based on skin color – that they had the superiority complex that most light-skinned people seemed to have. However, the overall environment in England made Natashia happy. People here did not seem to judge her for her dark skin, and Natashia felt she was living here without the invisible weight she always carried around on the island.

The time came when Natashia had to return to the island. Two days before her departure, she went to the mall and brought lots of school supplies that were way cheaper here than on the islands. Why couldn't her father send these supplies down and help Cece? Natashia wondered but knew better than to ask. She also brought some knickknacks for her cousins and a dress for Cece; all of that made for one hundred pounds.

Without making it quite obvious, Natashia had saved some of the money that Brad had given to her during her stay; for shopping and exploring the city. She knew that money would help her purchase her school textbooks. On the morning she left England, her dad handed her the ticket and her passport, but nothing more. He did not send any money with her, and she was not surprised.

His version of providing for his daughter was purchasing a flight ticket so that she could come to see how well he was doing in England and then return to a life of have-nots. Saying her goodbyes, she hopped on the plane, this time on her own. She couldn't say she missed her father, but she did miss the country where she had felt light and free like a bird.

On arriving at the airport on the island, she was greeted by her mother and Jack and Nancy as well as Aunt Mary. Natashia rushed into her mother's arms, who held her tightly. At that moment, she knew her mother had missed her as much as she had missed her. She also knew that Cece loved her, though she never expressed it openly with words.

"Hey, our turn now!" Nancy protested, when the embrace between mother and daughter went on too long for her liking.

Cece laughed and backed away. Natashia launched herself into her two cousins' open arms. Jack and Nancy hugged her tight, telling her how boring the summer was, without her there to pester them.

"Right, I know you missed me!" Natashia said confidently.

"We would have, but we never got the time to," Jack teased, conking her on her head.

Natashia made a face at him, but before she could retort, Aunt Mary told them to start walking out of the airport since their hired vehicle was waiting.

Natashia linked her arms with Nancy and began to walk outside. She looked at her family and realized how relieved and happy she felt to be with them after such a long separation. That day, Natashia understood that there was no place like home, and these people who loved her unconditionally were her home.

Chapter 11 – The Medical Student

Natashia had returned to the island with newfound wisdom on what the world outside of the island was really like. England was starkly different than the island, and she hadn't felt as belittled for her tar colored skin as she had, living on the island. Because the city was so big, people tended to mind their own business, and not worry about other people's issues and problems. She blended into the crowd, and she was so grateful to have had that experience.

However, coming home had been a blessing. She was glad she was reunited with her mother and the people who loved and cared for her wellbeing. Yet, the hustle and bustle of a big city with so many people who didn't seem to judge her or care so much for the color of her black skin gave her something new to think about. She began to delve into God's plan for her. She started to think of how God had intended for her to be dark-skinned for a reason and for a purpose, and she intended to figure out and understand that purpose later in life, as she grew older.

Since then, Natashia knew that it was the only thing that was now important to excel in life and the only way to live a better one. She studied harder than usual after that, not allowing herself to become consumed in things that other girls her age were invested in, such as conversing intimately with bus drivers, who were all men twice their age. When the final exams came around – the exams that determined the futures of everyone on the island – she ended up outshining most of her classmates by completing seven diplomas.

The next step that Natashia had to take in her life was finding a job and applying to a university. Her father, Brad, had started filing an application for her permanent residency in England. She was fully ready to embark on this journey to England and experience new things. The only thing she was sad about was that Cece would not be accompanying her.

When she got to England, her seven diplomas were not recognized, so that meant she had to attend community college. She was pleasantly surprised to find that there were several different ethnicities, such as Chinese, Koreans, Arabian, Hispanic, Africans, and many more at the community college. It made her feel less conscious of her own skin to see so many other people who were as dark if not had darker skin than her. She felt like she fit in a lot more in this environment. No one called each other names, and they treated each other the same. On the other hand, though, she was living with Brad's family - his wife would always belittle her. She couldn't understand why his wife didn't like her. Was it because of her complexion? Or was it because of the fact that she was growing closer to her father, much to his wife's dismay? Brad's wife would always try and dismantle their relationship by telling him lies and creating false gossip about Natashia.

The other thing she was struggling with was the fact that it was superbly cold here most of the year, which she was absolutely not used to because the island was usually warm all year round. Throughout the first year of moving to England, she stayed wrapped up in a bundle of clothes to keep herself warm.

She made a lot of friends in community college – one of whom was a Brazilian man named Solo. He was mostly white, but he never once called her names because of her complexion. He simply looked beyond the skin color of a person and looked at who they were on the inside, which is why he and Natashia fast became fast friends. People in her close circle of friends, as well as her family, had thought that she and Solo were dating. Several of her friends would often compliment her on her beauty, but she would brush it off because she knew that beauty came from having a fair complexion – which she did not have. After one year at the community college, she ventured into a degree of business administration because her friends were doing so, and she didn't want to lose them.

And then a strange thing happened to her one day in class at her new, career college. A boy stared at her from across the classroom with an unwavering glance. She could not for the life of her understand why he was staring at her, and instantly assumed that it was because he wanted to insult her. The boy had white skin with blue eyes and blonde hair.

All she could think about was how nervous she was getting because she had read about the KKK clan in her history class and wondered if the boy who was staring at her was one of the people from the clan. A string of panicked thoughts began going through her head, and she was so sure that this boy wanted to kidnap her and gang rape her – and when she thought this, the boy winked at her. She was wholly slumped and utterly confused because she couldn't for the life of her understand what this boy seemed to want with her.

At the end of the class, he walked over to her. *"Hey,"* he started, smiling at her. *"My name's Nike,"* he told her, holding out his hand for her to shake.

Natashia was at a total loss of words. She couldn't understand why this white boy was introducing himself, as if he had an interest in her. Nike, however, looked confused from her silence. *"I'm Nike,"* he repeated, slower this time.

"I'm Natashia," she replied in a shaky voice, not having much capacity to do anything else. Nike sat down next to Natashia and started talking with her. They spoke for almost an hour about Natashia's studies, and as the conversation came to a close because of Nike's class that was going to start soon, they even arranged to meet again the next day in study hall at the same time.

Though she was a little nervous, she met him the next day regardless. The same routine continued for three weeks until eventually, Nike asked out Natashia on a date. Natashia was extremely unused to the dating game and had no idea how it was supposed to go, so she went to Solo for advice. Solo encouraged her to go on a date and even offered to be her 'taxi.' However, she told him that Nike had said he would pick her up. She wondered what she would tell her father, and whether or not he would be okay with it. She hoped that he would because her half-brothers and sister had started dating from a young age. The day of the date, she told Nike that she would meet him down at the seven-eleven that was down the street from his house. Nike had gotten her a bouquet of roses and a box of chocolates for the date, and it made her immeasurably happy because she had never had someone to buy her chocolates and roses before.

He was extremely nice to her as they started dating, and she felt comfortable around him. He made her laugh when he told corny jokes, and he always complimented her by telling her that she was beautiful, and how much he loved her 'chocolate complexion.' She saw him as a shield to her dark, ebony complexion because it allowed her to hide behind his fairness.

As the relationship progressed, Nike would follow Natashia wherever she went. He began to grow extremely possessive and jealous, and this began to distress her greatly. She was unable to meet her friends, and her friendship with Solo was practically nonexistent in the course of her relationship with Nike. Although Nike took away the insecurities with her complexion for a bit and gave her a bit of an escape from it, their relationship was now growing toxic and unhealthy. Nike seemed to be obsessed with knowing where Natashia was at all times, and she felt suffocated by it. This led her to breaking things off with him. Living with her father in England had caused Natashia to have plenty of problems. She didn't drink or smoke, so when her friends went clubbing on Saturday nights, she would be put into the role of the designated driver. She got her driver's license at twenty and bought a used car with her savings from working at the Mall. She even bought herself a cellphone, and this also gave her a reason to stay out of the house more, as she was beginning to feel greatly unwelcomed in Brad's house.

She eventually found a solution to her living situation and moved in with a friend. This was, unfortunately, not an ideal living situation because she was having financial troubles. But eventually, her aunt offered Natashia to move in with her in her apartment that was quite close to her father's house, too, which she gratefully accepted as it made her financial situation a lot better. When Natashia would return to the island to visit her mother, she would often try to keep her out of the loop of her financial troubles and her problems with the relationship between her father and her. So instead, they would bask in the sun on the beach and relax by drinking coconut water. When she could call Cece once every month, she would always tell her that everything was fine. She didn't want to burden her mother with the weight of her problems or paint a beastly image of her father's wife.

"Everything's fine, mom. I'm doing well, Brad's good, and college is going well. It's all good," she would tell Cece over the phone.

After she had moved out of her father's house, he never called to check in on her or ask her if she was doing alright. This effectively put a halt to her and Brad's relationship altogether.

Natashia would take to praying and repenting and asking God to help her on her journey. She would often cry as she prayed with the passion with which she was asking God for help. Her circle of friends was beginning to fade away, and she was struggling a lot to keep herself together. She could not understand her purpose in life, and further than that, she was still struggling to come to terms with the color of her skin, not understanding what God intended when he gave her that skin color, where she was so black that she thought she resembled tar.

"Please, God, please help me find some understanding. Some meaning. I just want to understand what I am supposed to do. Help me!" She would pray in desperation. By some lucky coincidence, she met a man at the church. He was tall and light-skinned, and he had a passion for God. His name was John, and he was in pre-med. He and Natashia dated for six months until he asked her to marry him. Marrying him was one of the most important decisions of her life. The wedding was attended by only close friends and family, and it was absolutely beautiful.

After two years of being married to John, he had to leave for medical school in Chicago, while she stayed in England to complete her degree. When she graduated with an associate degree in business Administration, she landed a clerical position at a firm in Rochester, England, where she worked for six years. However, she decided that this was not the right course for her. The decision to switch fields hadn't been made suddenly – Natashia's aunt dies of cancer, and her death empowered Natashia to make a difference, and so, she too decided to pursue medicine like her husband. By God's blessing, she managed to get student loans and register for medical school in Chicago alongside John.

Chapter 12 – Home

In Natashia's second year of medical school, she encountered a significant number of financial problems. She had to make the tough decision of asking her father if he could lend her some money for her tuition. After her wedding to John, she occasionally called her father to ask how he was doing, but he never called her first. She was the one who was always trying to make an effort, and it never came from his side.

The conversation they had about money was the most awkward one Natashia had ever had with him to date. She had called him one night after a desperate attempt at looking through each of her bank accounts, and the money needed to complete her second year but finding no answers.

"Hey, Dad," she started after he had picked up the phone.

"Hello, Natashia, how are you?" he had asked in return, not really sounding that enthusiastic, but being kind in his response regardless.

She decided not to beat around the bush and get right to it, as there was no reason to stall the conversation. *"Not so great,"* she replied solemnly. *"I'm having some financial trouble ... I was hoping you could send me some money for my tuition, so I could pay for my second year of medical school,"* she said, her voice slightly hopeful.

"Oh," was all her father replied. Then, there was silence. He seemed to be deliberating the best way to turn her down because there was static on his end of the phone for several long moments. *"The truth is, Natashia,"* he said finally. *"I don't have much money, really. Most of it is gone, and I can't really afford to waste the remaining on other things."*

Waste it. Right! That's what her father considered was worth her education. They tried to fill in the awkwardness that followed after the rejection of his response, but it just felt like she was trying too hard to talk to a man, who had basically told her a lie. She knew quite well that he had money. He had just purchased five acres of land only recently. They hung up soon afterward.

This was too much of a disappointment for her, and she wasn't sure why she thought it wouldn't be a disappointment when she made the phone call in the first place. It was a big mistake, and she regretted it immensely. She ended up not being able to afford her second year after all, and after more desperate attempts at finding money to pay her tuition bills with, she decided to ultimately take the year off and save up. John's stipend in his residency was not enough to pay for her third year in medical school either, so she worked in that time at the hospital as a food assistant. Within time, though, the money she was making from the hospital was not enough, so she had bake sales at the church and asked for donations from church members.

With the grace of God and the graciousness of the church members who lent a hand, she was able to save up three thousand dollars in savings for her tuition for medical school. She continued her studies, despite things getting worse for her financially. But she prayed to God regularly to help her find a way to finish because she desperately wanted to make an impact and serve the community.

She was also beginning to realize more and more about how her skin color didn't matter as much as she had initially believed. It wasn't as significant as she made it seem. She began to research black icons in history, who had found a way to change the future despite the color of their skin. She began to feel more and more proud to wear the skin color that she had and was given by God. In England, she never had to deal with racism, but in America, people were more racist and against certain things and ideas. However, this was not the case in England, where people minded their own business and didn't judge other people for the way that they looked, which made her return to England with excitement. She was looking forward to meeting her friends, especially Solo, whom she had not caught up within a while. The last time she had met him, he had gotten married and had a baby girl, but unfortunately, the marriage to his Mexican wife didn't work out, and they got divorced. Two years before Natashia had married John, she had visited the island to meet her mother. They would sit on the beach, eating mangoes and recalling childhood stories.

On the same trip back to the island, she met her high school classmates for a reunion. She was shocked to find out that most of them had changed their ways and were no longer calling her nasty names, but rather, complimenting her on her appearance. This came as a huge shocker to Natashia because it felt strange to hear such niceties coming from her former bullies, rather than the onslaught of insults that usually accompanied them whenever they saw her. They gave her positive compliments about her skin color, telling her that her complexion had lightened considerably and that she had grown to be quite beautiful. She even found the courage to confront one of her former bullies.

"Why did you always bully me about my complexion and have so much hatred toward me? Why did you always call me blackbird?" she asked her bravely.

The bully couldn't respond to the question appropriately because she didn't have a proper answer. She simply shrugged after taking a moment to think about it. *"We were young, and we didn't know any better. I really don't know,"* she said, looking genuinely ashamed and guilty, as well as a little fumbled by the question in the first place.

Upon hearing this, Natashia was actually a little relieved. She used to honestly think there was something wrong with her growing up that made everyone hate her. Knowing now, there was nothing of the sort, it made her feel a lot better. She was also able to find it in her heart to forgive her bully, even though she never actually apologized for her crude remarks that she made as a child.

After that, Natashia spent the rest of her trip visiting the island, eating mangoes on the beach with Cece, not used to the hot weather again. When she had to eventually leave, she was extremely sad about having to leave Cece behind while she pursued her dreams.

In her fourth year of medical school, there was less of a financial strain on Natashia. Her husband, John, was nearly done with his residency and was working as a surgeon at one of the local hospitals in Chicago. From time to time, she would still call her father and ask him about his wellbeing, trying to be genuine when she talked to him, in a great effort to forget her haunting past. But, much to her dismay, it kept creeping back up to her and forcing her to relive the endless amount of times that she was let down and disappointed. However, she powered through it by making God the center of her life.

Natashia and John found a new passion, which was traveling. They greatly enjoyed going to a different place, and interacting in a different culture, learning about the customs of that area. They started missions with small church groups and would visit areas that needed medical attention to give them assistance with what they required. The first place they visited was Papua New Guinea, and they stayed there for three weeks. The people in Papua New Guinea were also dark-skinned, but they were proud of their way of life, as well as the color of their skin. They lived a simple life, not needing the pleasure of television or investing in the lives of people in Hollywood.

The people lived in wooden houses, and they were genuinely happy with the life they had built for themselves. No child had a frown on their face; they were all smiling. Natashia was in charge of helping the children by cooking, singing, and using the four years of medical school expertise with physical examination assistance. John, on the other hand, was responsible for performing minor surgeries and different types of medical procedures. There was no big hospital within the immediate island, it was a few hours away. All they had was a small clinic where they would host checkups. People would use herbal remedies, and some even worshipped their ancestors.

Natashia's eagerness to help people in need was fueled further in this country. She would think less about herself and the burden she carried with her deep insecurity about her skin color and thought more about other people and her willingness to help them. The people on the island were not bothered by their skin color or dark babies, they showed each other equal respect and were obedient to their elders. The people from Papua New Guinea gave Natashia a new outlook on life, and she found that the problems that she had on her own island growing up, financially, emotionally, and physically were practically insignificant compared to what other people in the world were going through. The three weeks she and John spent there was a riveting experience, and Natashia found that getting time away to spend with John on the island and indulging in the many varieties of fruit they had to offer was a pleasant escape and doubled as a form of relaxation as well. They left the island feeling changed, and Natashia had gained a new power of belief that she held the ability to change her life and make things better.

John and Natashia became frequently involved in taking trips all around the world after that, going to their next mission in Africa to the country of Sudan. In Sudan, people were different. Whether it was because of the language barrier or because of the devastation of war, people were more silent here. They seemed to have a familiar look in their eyes that said, *"Why do we have to suffer at the hands of someone else?"*

Natashia would teach a class there with the help of a translator, and each morning, when she got to class, she would hug every child in the room. Within a few days, the children's faces began to light up, and she was so grateful to have played a part in that. It gave her hope. She would talk to the children about Bible stories and tell them about how Jesus used to have children around him all the time. Natashia felt at ease in Sudan because people were extremely dark-skinned there, which gave her some perspective on how other people in the world lived. They, too, did not judge people based on the color of their skin and seemed comfortable with the way that they looked. It gave her a sense of comfort, and she didn't have to think about how she felt about her own color. However, the war had begun to escalate, so she and John had to leave the country. They spent two days in Ghana after that, where the culture in that place evolved them.

They learned about the history of slavery, and how, on some level, it was still imminent within the country. It gave her a newfound appreciation for her background because even though she was as dark-skinned as charcoal – not fair-skinned like her parents or the rest of the people back on the island – at least, she was never put through a slave trade because of it. It gave her the will to forgive her bullies for the agony they had caused her in her life. It also gave her the strength to finally put the insecurities of her skin color to a close, and she stopped continually dwelling on the fact that she was black. Eventually, though, Natashia had to get back to her residency program, and John was getting limited time off work, so their mission trips were put on hold.

The residency was not easy, and she had to work hard, with almost twenty-four hours a day shift. Cece was very proud of the work that Natashia was doing, so much so that she was telling people about all of the things that she was doing. In turn, Natashia was making sure that Cece was well taken care of, so she would continue to make her proud. Natashia's stringent residency program was beginning to take a toll on her, and she was starting to get exhausted and stressed because of it. She had to rely heavily on her husband for help, and she prayed every night to God to give her the strength to get through it.

There was an incident in the ICU that further propelled her new outlook on life. While she was tending to a two-year-old who was nursing a minor concussion, the head preceptor began shouting and disparaging at Natashia, questioning her ability to do her job. She was nervous because of the observers in the room, feeling belittled and degraded in the way that the man had shot her down. However, she had still managed to stabilize the two-year-old, despite the pressure that was on her. Feeling humiliated, she went to the doctor after her shift was over, and in a fury, said to him, *"Don't ever shout at me again."*

The preceptor was shocked because he had not perceived Natashia as someone to react or defend herself. But, the next day during rounds, he publicly apologized to Natashia. This gave her a sense of relief, as she had believed this incident would lead to her being expelled from the program. Except now, she did not care so much about her skin complexion and was evolving into garnering a superior attitude and view herself as important. Every day, she would wake up in the morning and look at herself in the mirror and repeat one thing to herself:

"No one is better than me." Even on the days she felt otherwise.

John eventually began to work long shifts and got little time on weekends, yet they always made sure to spend quality time together. When her residency program ended, she and John made plans to spend some time with his family. Natashia had liked John's family a lot. They had always been quite friendly and welcoming to her and treated her like she was one of their own. She even called his parents 'mom' and 'dad.'

John and his father had a very special bond, and he greatly valued his presence in his life. His father would always encourage them to excel in life and be the best they could.

Chapter 13 – Robert

Several years ago, Natashia had begun to feel nauseous and suspect that she was pregnant. Her suspicions were correct – she was pregnant with a boy. When the baby was born, she and John decided to name him Robert, after John's late father. When Robert was born, Natashia was at a point in her life where she was entirely at peace. So much so that when she was pregnant, she had actually hoped that her baby would be as dark as her.

The world was changing, and people were starting to see dark skin and people of color as beautiful too. The baby wouldn't even have to face the same obstacles that she had met, growing up on the island. Where they lived now, people were more accustomed to seeing dark-skinned people and were considerably more accepting of it than the people that Natashia grew up with on the island.

When the baby came, he was actually light-skinned, but to Natashia, it didn't matter. She loved him even if he was light and didn't care about his skin color. Natashia and John were looking forward to being the best parents they could be. Robert even looked like his namesake, and for that, John was delighted. Robert was a considerably quiet child. Natashia and John were very excited to spend time with him and raise him, as he had quickly become their number one priority. They always made sure that Robert knew he was loved and talked to him often about the man he was named after, telling him about all the great ways that he would live.

Slowly and surely, Natashia was becoming more and more comfortable in her skin and the way she looked. She was delighted to find that more and more people were becoming aware of the beauty that lied in dark skin and finding colored people to be extremely beautiful. She was incredibly proud to see a Sudanese model with dark skin on the cover of a very popular magazine.

It filled her with pride at the knowledge that the people from one of her and John's previous trips to Sudan were considered to be so beautiful. She no longer felt like her skin color was something to be ashamed of, and she was growing more and more proud of the way she looked, not fearing that it was something to be concerned about. She no longer felt like it was something that she needed to hide from and change about herself. It was now something that she could be proud of and embrace openly.

When Robert turned six years old, John was offered a job in Florida. The small family was looking forward to the move, especially Robert who was excited to visit Disney World. Cece was also coming to Florida to spend more time with the family, and for that, Natashia was excited. Soon, Natashia also got a job that was relatively close to where John worked. She and John made sure to still find time to go to church and introduce Robert to church as well.

John's mother was also quite close to Robert. She was also his babysitter, and she was so attached to him that he spent much time with her and didn't get to meet other children from church, at the park, or even at birthdays. When he started grade one, he didn't feel comfortable being there alone and didn't want to go, which led to Natashia having to spend the day with him, helping him to get comfortable.

However, after two weeks, Robert was more comfortable going to school and would come home, telling his parents stories about his classmates, and the things he did that day. John and Natashia had admitted Robert into a school with predominantly colored children. He would come home on some days and ask why he was not as dark-skinned as his classmates or his mother. He wanted to fit in but was ignored by most of his classmates.

When he began third grade, he was bullied for having light skin, as compared to the rest of his classmates and would come home very distressed about it. Natashia had to sit him down and talk to him about bullying eventually.

"Why can't I have skin like yours?" Robert said, distressed after his mother made him sit down across from her. *"All the other kids bully me and call me white boy."*

"When I was growing up," Natashia began to tell him. *"People would make fun of my skin."*

The young boy's eyes widened comically.

"Really?" He squeaked in surprise.

He was shocked that his mother had gone through something similar for the very thing that he wanted. While he got bullied for having light skin, Natashia had gotten bullied for having dark skin. It was a weird thing to digest.

"Yes," she told him calmly. *"They would call me terrible names like 'blackbird' and other mean things."*

Robert took a second to grasp that knowledge before blinking several times.

"What did you do?" He asked her. *"Did you hit them?"*

"No, I didn't hit them," she said. *"Hitting is not okay. I cried a lot and always felt sad to be dark-skinned, but I had to learn to accept myself, and the way I looked. It took me a long, long time to accept my skin color."*

"Will I ever be able to accept my skin color?" He asked.

"Of course, you will. It may take time, but I do not doubt in my mind you will get there. You are a beautiful boy, and mommy and daddy love you very, very much. So do your grandmothers! I will remind you every day how handsome you are so that you never forget it. Everyone is just jealous of your creamy complexion and wish that it belonged to them," she said to him.

She spent a long time teaching Robert to embrace his skin color and be confident in how he looked. She worked very hard with him in trying to boost his self-esteem, so he would not suffer the same way that she did when she was growing up. Natashia and John even talked about moving Robert from his current school into a school where there was predominantly white-skinned students. However, after further discussion, they decided to keep him where he was, and instead, help him overcome the insecurities and his self-esteem issues.

John figured that if he was bullied here at his school for having light skin, it was possible that even at a school with other white children, he would be bullied by them too in some way or other. So, it was just easier and simpler to keep him where he was. After that, Natashia went to Robert's school for a parent-teacher meeting and addressed the issue with the teachers and the principal. They all agreed that this bullying would not be tolerated and that they would take this offense seriously and start enforcing a zero-tolerance policy for bullying at their school.

Their seriousness in taking control of the matter made her secretly wish in envy that a teacher might have stood up for her in the same way when she was in school. Still, at the end of the day, she was quite glad that the teachers were taking a stand for her son. Robert was her son, and she did not want him to be burdened with the same scars that she had, growing up.

John, Natashia, and Robert started to go on more mission trips in all parts of the world and really enjoyed doing that together as a family. She was proud that she had raised Robert in such a way that one of his favorite pastimes was helping other people. They visited many places, met lots of different people, and were exposed to several cultures. They were happy with their little family, perfectly content in their lives and with how far they had come together. There was no more of any bitterness or self-hatred stored inside Natashia. She was able to move forward in her life, ready to face what was to come, with the help of her family and the strength of God.

Dark as the depth of the earth and polish in charcoal cream

Eyes as bright and shiny as the farthest star in the galaxy

Voice as soft as jellyfish

Hair is thick, black and curly, shaped like a trapezoid

She looks lost in her thoughts

Thinking of the day when darkness was a curse, a shame to look upon

But the light has shone as darkness, and it has become a sapphire

Radiating in the atmosphere,

Not wanting to be recognized

But her swarthiness took the breath of her passerby.

She bent her head in dismay,

And her only thought was her darkness, what is so wrong with this color.

www.ingramcontent.com/pod-product-compliance
Lightning Source LLC
Chambersburg PA
CBHW030826090426
42737CB00009B/894